MW00989373

Praise for Michael E. Gerber, Anthony C. Bass, and *The E-Myth Landscape Contractor*

I have known Tony Bass for years. **I have enjoyed seeing Tony turn a small landscape company into an extremely profitable and successful company with the application of these principles.** I have the highest respect for his advice and consider him a valuable asset to the entire landscape industry.

Charles Vander Kooi, author; speaker

No one else offers such practical and applicable knowledge that I can use today to make my business and my life a great success!

David Bower, president, 7 Oaks Landscaping

When your back hurts, when you are tired of working sixty to eighty hours a week, when you are fed up with doing everything yourself and are ready to make serious money in the lawn and landscaping business, you need to read this book. Next, simply do what Tony and Michael say. Your future success depends on it!

Richard Bare, president and founder, Arbor-nomics

In my opinion, Tony Bass is an expert at creating systems for the landscape industry. **Tony has helped my company earn double-digit profitability by putting these very systems into place.** Can you afford to take a risk and buy this book? You cannot afford not to!

Troy Rhone, owner, Integrity Landscapes; owner, Troy Rhone
Garden Design; garden editor, *Flower* magazine

All contractors should read this book if they desire to have more control over their lives and businesses. Thinking, planning, and acting with the end in mind is the message that Tony and Michael provide in this incredibly insightful book. If you plan on building long-term wealth and would like to have control over your future financial options, then read this book and share it with your friends and family.

Doug Robbins, Robbins Landscaping; national award-winning contractor

Tony Bass addresses all the issues we face as landscape contractors, and he does it with dirt under his fingernails. He is one of us! **The ideas, tools, and extremely valuable knowledge that Tony provides in this book will give you and your company the confidence to tackle everything, from planning your financial future to managing your employees' daily routines.**

Landon Wise, Wyscape Landscaping Contractors

Michael Gerber's *E-Myth* is one of only four books I recommend as required reading. **For those looking to start and build a business of their own, this is the man who has coached more successful entrepreneurs than the next ten gurus combined.**

Timothy Ferris, #1 *New York Times* best-selling author, *The 4-Hour Workweek*

Everyone needs a mentor, someone who tells it like it is, holds you accountable, and shows you your good, bad, and ugly. For millions of small-business owners, Michael Gerber is that person. Let Michael be your mentor and you are in for a kick in the pants, the ride of a lifetime.

John Jantsch, author, *Duct Tape Marketing*

Michael Gerber is a master instructor and a leader's leader. As a combat F15 fighter pilot, I had to navigate complex missions with life-and-death consequences, but until I read *The E-Myth* and met Michael Gerber, my transition to the world of small business was a nightmare with no real flight plan. **The hands-on, practical magic of Michael's turnkey systems magnified by the raw power of his keen insight and wisdom have changed my life forever.**

Steve Olds, CEO, Stratworx.com

Michael Gerber's strategies in *The E-Myth* were instrumental in building my company from two employees to a global organization; I can't wait to see how applying the strategies from *Awakening the Entrepreneur Within* will affect its growth!

Dr. Ivan Misner, founder and chairman, BNI; author, *Masters of Sales*

Michael Gerber's gift to isolate the issues and present simple, direct, business-changing solutions shines bright with *Awakening the Entrepreneur Within*. **If you're interested in developing an entrepreneurial vision and plan that inspires others to action, buy this book, read it, and apply the processes Gerber brilliantly defines.**

Tim Templeton, author, *The Referral of a Lifetime*

Michael Gerber truly, truly understands what it takes to be a successful practicing entrepreneur and business owner. He has demonstrated to me over six years of working with him that for those who stay the course and learn much more than just "how to work on their business and not in it" then they will reap rich rewards. **I finally franchised my business, and the key to unlocking this kind of potential in any business is the teachings of Michael's work.**

Chris Owen, marketing director, Royal Armouries (International) PLC

Michael's work has been an inspiration to us. **His books have helped us get free from the out-of-control life that we once had. His no-nonsense approach kept us focused on our ultimate aim rather than day-to-day stresses. He has helped take our business to levels we couldn't have imagined possible.** In the Dreaming Room made us totally reevaluate how we thought about our business and our life. We have now redesigned our life so we can manifest the dreams we unearthed in Michael's Dreaming Room.

Jo and Steve Davison, founders, The Spinal Health Clinic
Chiropractic Group and www.your-dream-life.com

Because of Michael Gerber, I transformed my twenty-four-hour-a-day, seven-day-a-week job (also called a small business) into a multi-million dollar turnkey business. This in turn set the foundation for my worldwide training firm. **I am living my dream because of Michael Gerber.**

Howard Partridge, Phenomenal Products Inc.

Michael Gerber is an outrageous revolutionary who is changing the way the world does business. **He dares you to commit to your grandest dreams and then shows you how to make the impossible a reality. If you let him, this man will change your life.**

Fiona Fallon, founder, Divine and The Bottom Line

Michael Gerber is a genius. Every successful business person I meet has read Michael Gerber, refers to Michael Gerber, and lives by his words. You just can't get enough of Michael Gerber. **He has the innate (and rare) ability to tap into one's soul, look deeply, and tell you what you need to hear. And then, he inspires you, equips you with the tools to get it done.**

Pauline O'Malley, CEO, TheRevenueBuilder

When asked, "Who was the most influential person in your life?" I am one of the thousands who don't hesitate to say "Michael E. Gerber." **Michael helped transform me from someone dreaming of retirement to someone dreaming of working until age one hundred.** This awakening is the predictable outcome of anyone reading Michael's new book.

Thomas O. Bardeen

Michael Gerber is an incredible business philosopher, guru, perhaps even a seer. He has an amazing intuition, which allows him to see in an instant what everybody else is missing; he sees opportunity everywhere. **While in the Dreaming Room, Michael gave me the gift of seeing through the eyes of an awakened entrepreneur, and instantly my business changed from a regional success to serving clients on four continents.**

Keith G. Schiehl, president, Rent-a-Geek Computer Services

Michael Gerber is among the very few who truly understand entrepreneurship and small business. While others talk about these topics in the form of theories, methodologies, processes, and so on, Michael goes to the heart of the issues. **Whenever Michael writes about entrepreneurship, soak it in as it is not only good for your business, but great for your soul.** His words will help you to keep your passion and balance while sailing through the uncertain sea of entrepreneurship.

Raymond Yeh, co-author, *The Art of Business*

Michael Gerber forced me to think big, think real, and gave me the support network to make it happen. A new wave of entrepreneurs is rising, much in thanks to his amazing efforts and very practical approach to doing business.

Christian Kessner, founder, Higher Ground Retreats and Events

Michael's understanding of entrepreneurship and small business management has been a difference maker for countless businesses, including Infusion Software. **His insights into the entrepreneurial process of building a business are a must-read for every small business owner.** The vision, clarity, and leadership that came out of our Dreaming Room experience were just what our company needed to recognize our potential and motivate the whole company to achieve it.

Clate Mask, president and CEO, Infusion Software

Michael Gerber is a truly remarkable man. His steady openness of mind and ability to get to the deeper level continues to be an inspiration and encouragement to me. **He seems to always ask that one question that forces the new perspective to break open and he approaches the new coming method in a fearless way.**

Rabbi Levi Cunin, Chabad of Malibu

The Dreaming Room experience was literally life changing for us. **Within months, we were able to start our foundation and make several television appearances owing to his teachings.** He has an incredible charisma, which is priceless, but above all Michael Gerber *awakens* passion from within, enabling you to take action with dramatic results . . . starting today!

Shona and Shaun Carcary, Trinity Property
Investments Inc. — Home Vestors franchises

I thought *E-Myth* was an awkward name! What could this book do for me? **But when I finally got to reading it . . . it was what I was looking for all along.** Then, to top it off, I took a twenty-seven-hour trip to San Diego just to attend the Dreaming Room, where Michael touched my heart, my mind, and my soul.

Helmi Natto, president, Eye 2 Eye Optics, Saudi Arabia

I attended In the Dreaming Room and was challenged by Michael Gerber to "Go out and do what's impossible." So I did. **I became an author and international speaker and used Michael's principles to create a world-class company that will change and save lives all over the world.**

Dr. Don Kennedy, MBA; author, *5 AM & Already Behind*, www.bahbits.com

I went to the Dreaming Room to have Michael Gerber fix my business. He talked about Dreaming. What was this Dreaming? I was too busy working! Too busy being miserable, angry, frustrated, behind in what I was trying to accomplish. And losing everything I was working for. **Then Michael Gerber woke up the dreamer in me and remade my life and my business.**

Pat Doorn, president, Mountain View Electric Ltd.

Michael Gerber can captivate a room full of entrepreneurs and take them to a place where they can focus on the essentials that are the underpinning of every successful business. He gently leads them from where they are to where they need to be in order to change the world.

Francine Hardaway, CEO, Stealthmode Partners; founder,
the Arizona Entrepreneurship Conferences

The E Myth

Landscape Contractor

*Why Most Landscape
Companies Don't Work
and What to Do About It*

MICHAEL E. GERBER

ANTHONY C. BASS

PRODIGY
BUSINESS BOOKS

Published by
Prodigy Business Books, Inc., Carlsbad, California.

Production Team
Patricia A. Beaulieu, chief operating officer, book division manager, Prodigy Business Books, Inc.; Helen Chang, editor, helenchangwriter.com; Erich Broesel, cover designer, BroeselDesign, Inc.; Nancy Ratkiewich, book production, njr productions; Jeff Kassebaum, Michael E. Gerber author photographer, Jeff Kassebaum and Co.; Steve Schroeder, Tony Bass author photographer, Steve Schroeder Photography

Copyright
Copyright © 2011 Michael E. Gerber. All rights reserved. No part of this publication may be reproduced, stored in a retrieval system, or transmitted in any form or by any means, electronic, mechanical, photocopying, recording, scanning, or otherwise, except as permitted under Section 107 or 108 of the 1976 United States Copyright Act, without either the prior written permission of the Publisher. Requests to the Publisher for permission should be addressed to Prodigy Business Books, Inc., P.O. Box 131195, Carlsbad, CA, 92013.

Limit of Liability/Disclaimer of Warranty; While the publisher and authors have used their best efforts in preparing this book, they make no representations or warranties with respect to the accuracy or completeness of the contents of this book and specifically disclaim any implied warranties of merchantability or fitness for a particular purpose. No warranty may be created or extended by sales representative or written sales materials. The advice and strategies contained herein may not be suitable for your situation. You should consult with a professional where appropriate. Neither the publisher nor the authors shall be liable for any loss of profit or any other commercial damages, including but not limited to special, incidental, consequential, or other damages.

For general information on other products and services, please visit the website: www.michaelegerber.com.

ISBN 978-0-9835001-6-2 (pbk)
ISBN 978-0-9835001-7-9 (cloth)
ISBN 978-0-9835542-3-3 (ebk)

Printed in the United States of America

10 9 8 7 6 5 4 3 2 1

To Luz Delia, whose heart expands mine,
whose soul inspires mine,
whose boldness reaches for the stars, thank you,
forever, for being, truly mine...

—Michael E. Gerber

CONTENTS

A WORD ABOUT THIS BOOK

Michael E. Gerber

My first E-Myth book was published in 1985. It was called *The E-Myth: Why Most Small Businesses Don't Work and What to Do About It.* Since that book, and the company I created to provide business development services to its many readers, millions have read *The E-Myth*, and the book that followed it called *The E-Myth Revisited*, and tens of thousands have participated in our E-Myth Mastery programs.

The co-author of this book, Tony Bass, was one of those people who read my book many years ago, but I had never met. Tony contacted me recently to connect, and after hearing his story, we decided to collaborate on this book. His successful landscape contracting business is a direct result of his enthusiasm and the deliberate application of the principles set forward in my E-Myth books. What a wonderful, powerful example of organizing for growth, for the many entrepreneurs, new and old, in his field!

This book is two things: the product of my lifelong work conceiving, developing, and growing the E-Myth way into a business model that has been applied to every imaginable kind of company in the world, as well as a product of Tony's extraordinary experience and success in applying the E-Myth to the development of his equally extraordinary enterprise, Super Lawn Technologies, Inc.

So it was that one day, while sitting with my muse, which I think of as my inner voice, and which many who know me think of as "here he goes again!" I thought about the creation of an entire series of E-Myth Expert books. That series, including this book, would be co-authored by experts in every industry who had successfully applied my E-Myth principles to the extreme development of a sole proprietorship—an employer plus one—with the intent of growing it nationwide, and even worldwide, which is what Tony had in mind as he began to discover the almost infinite range of opportunities provided by thinking the E-Myth way.

Upon seeing the possibilities of this new idea, I immediately invited co-authors such as Tony to join me. They said, "Let's do it!" and so we did.

Welcome to *The E-Myth Landscape Contractor: Why Most Landscape Companies Don't Work and What to Do About It.*

Read it, enjoy it, and let us—Tony and I—help you apply the E-Myth to the re-creation, development, and extreme growth of your landscaping company into an enterprise that you can be justifiably proud of.

To your life, your wisdom, and the life and success of your clients, I wish you good reading.

—Michael E. Gerber
Co-Founder/Chairman
Michael E. Gerber Companies, Inc.
Carlsbad, California
www.michaelegerber.com/co-author

A NOTE FROM TONY

I retired at forty-one years old. That's twenty-four years earlier than the government suggests you retire.

I sat on the beach soaking up sunshine and watching my young children play in the waves. My beautiful wife, Lynn, stunning in her swimsuit, silently took photos for the family album. I was surrounded by my whole family of fourteen—my mom and dad, sisters, brothers-in-law, and nieces and nephews.

Our two-week-long family vacation was just getting started. I silently began to give thanks to a list of people who had helped me get there. I had just realized the ultimate American dream; this vacation could continue indefinitely.

My journey started nineteen years earlier when I had just returned from another two-week-long beach vacation—a present to myself for accomplishing my goal of graduating in exactly four years from the University of Georgia with a bachelor's degree in agricultural mechanization.

My plan had always been to get a degree, and then get a great paying job. But I made an unexpected announcement to my parents:

"Mom, Dad, I have made my decision. I'm going to be a businessman. And I would like to get my old room back for a while. I'll be moving back home."

My dad said, "Fine with me. Here's a coupon book. You can make the payments on your final school loan, Mr. Businessman."

My mom said, "What about the job at the grocery store? I thought you said they would hire you full time after you graduate?"

"Well, Mom, here's how I figure it. You guys let me move back in for a while. I have no family to support and very little expenses. This is the perfect time for me to start a business. If I fail, I hurt no one. If it works out, I'll make a lot of money."

"What kind of business?" my dad asked.

"I've been doing some research while at the university. My turfgrass professor says there's going to be a lot going on in the landscape industry the next couple of decades. I've been reading these land-scaping business magazines at the library. People are concerned about environmental stewardship. They also want their properties to look beautiful and will actually pay you to plant and mow lawns, plant trees, and even install sprinkler systems. I'm going to start a landscaping business. Look around town, because there are lots of housing projects going on."

My mom said, "Can you still keep your grocery store job part time?"

I always had love and support from my mom and dad, but they just couldn't comprehend the entrepreneurial life. I was respectful but undeterred by their skepticism.

It took five years of operating my small landscaping business for me to reach the next level in my entrepreneurial development. By that time, I was an accomplished technician with a significant port-folio of completed projects to prove it.

However, my business was in a crisis. I had a lot to lose. My wife was not happy with the amount of money I was bringing home or the number of hours I worked. I had more than one hundred accounts, but I also had commitments to the bank for equipment purchases and building costs for a small office. Plus, I had nine employees. Each had a family of his own. Life! Work! Business?

What went wrong? My plan was to make a lot of money. I asked myself why it was that every time I added a third working crew, things began to fall apart. How in the world could more work equal less pay? Why couldn't my employees do the work correctly? Why was I the only one who could make the schedule? And now that my landscape architect (a high school and college friend) had announced he was leaving, who would draw the plans?

And the estimates—nearly 300 estimates that last year. I couldn't write 300 estimates and run the field and do payroll and return calls and find the next employee. And besides all this, my back hurt from jumping up and down on a shovel for five years.

Business? Am I a businessman? Is this what I had dreamed about while lying on the beach after I graduated?

I had an idea. Perhaps the university didn't teach me everything I needed to know. Perhaps, just perhaps, I needed more education. But not horticulture, turfgrass, or landscape design. Perhaps there was somebody who could teach me how to run my small business.

I can't remember if I read about the book in one of my landscaping magazines or if I simply found it at the bookstore. But I found it: *The E-Myth: Why Most Small Businesses Don't Work and What to Do About It*. Reading this book changed everything for me. I had been working very hard, but the simple problem was that I was doing the wrong work.

Let me be clear. *The E-Myth* did not immediately solve my problems. But I achieved clarity by learning how to redefine, repurpose, and reinvent my small landscaping business. The book that cost less than twenty dollars became my blueprint for personal business activities, or how I spent my minutes, hours and days.

When I sat on the beach, retired at forty-one years old, silently giving thanks to those who had helped me along the way, there was one person on that list I had never met: Michael E. Gerber, the author of that little book, *The E-Myth*. It had been fourteen years since I had read the book. Was he even still alive?

The unfulfilled thank-you was more than I could stand. So I went online to look him up. I placed a phone call to his office. I wanted to simply say, "Thank you for your help, inspiration, and insight. Thank you, Mr. Michael E. Gerber, for helping me to achieve my dreams."

I was twenty-seven years old when I read *The E-Myth*. This was before e-mail, e-commerce, and E! Entertainment were mainstream words. This was even before *The E-Myth Revisited*. Today's budding entrepreneurs may see some level of conflict of clarity of the phrase.

But for me, the funny title was not the big deal. The sub-title made it clear: *Why Most Small Businesses Don't Work and What to Do About It.*

What had totally confused me at twenty-seven years old was a radical statement found inside that book that I could not comprehend, discuss, or even really seriously contemplate for a few minutes: "The only reason to start a business is to *sell* it one day."

Inside *The E-Myth* there were many guiding words that organized my thoughts into ideas, which led to specific actions that netted positive results. Words. Simple, powerful, helpful words.

Bad news: After reading *The E-Myth*, I knew instantly that my landscape company was incapable of growing. I instantly knew that I had to make radical changes. I owned a broken landscape company.

Good news: I instantly knew that I had an action plan that could change everything in the future. I had a new vision for my future landscape business.

So I took the next six months off from working in my business, and for six glorious months, which I called my sabbatical, I worked on my business.

I felt like I was back at the university working on a project, but this was much different. This project to reinvent my business had serious financial potential. This project had serious life potential.

Michael E. Gerber's words were etched into my brain. When there was a roadblock, or a lack of clarity, I retrieved the dog-eared book once again. These words guided my actions to work on my business for the next fourteen years, until I sold it for a nice seven-figure profit.

I started with nothing but my mom and dad's blessing. No money. No equipment. No practical experience. And today, here is my reality.

Entrepreneurism is the way to build wealth. And yes, you can make all the money you and your family will ever need in the landscaping business. I am living proof.

When I called Michael E. Gerber to say thank-you for the help, not only did I find out he was alive, I found out he was accelerating his outreach to entrepreneurs worldwide. Gerber's exact words from my notes: "Tony, I am working in it, while I am working on it." So we kept in touch with the occasional e-mail.

Now here we are, with *The E-Myth Landscape Contractor: Why Most Landscape Companies Don't Work and What to Do About It*. You hold in your hands the guiding words to organize your thoughts, and to guide your specific actions. You will quickly gain understanding of how to turn these specific actions into profitable, life-enhancing results.

If you are reading this, you are likely in the landscaping business, or you have a family member in the landscape business. Perhaps you're seriously thinking about starting your own landscaping business, or you work at a landscaping company. And regardless of where you are in the industry today, one day you will leave that business.

What Michael E. Gerber and I are doing here is trying to help you make sure that when you leave it, you have the greatest chance possible to enhance your family financially and emotionally. You do not have to work the next fifteen, twenty, thirty, or forty years and leave your family with a pile of bills, a mountain of used equipment to sell, and clients who have to find your replacement.

Every day I talk with owners of landscaping companies. I love talking to entrepreneurs. Most of them are simply trying to make a better living than the job they quit or the job they are thinking about quitting. However, there are a great number who are seeking information to improve, grow, expand, and accelerate their results. And for these business owners, I have great news.

Your landscaping business can be your ticket to financial prosperity. But better yet, your landscaping business can be your ticket to life prosperity. Remember, it will be much easier if you do certain things in a certain way. Let's call it *The E-Myth* way.

Enjoy your business! Enjoy your family! Enjoy life!

God bless,

Tony Bass

—Tony Bass
Founder/CEO
Super Lawn Technologies, Inc.
Fort Valley, Georgia
www.superlawntechnologies.com

PREFACE

Michael E. Gerber

I am not a landscape contractor, though I have helped dozens of landscape contractors reinvent their landscaping companies over the past thirty-five years.

I like to think of myself as a thinker, maybe even a dreamer. Yes, I like to *do* things. But before I jump in and get my hands dirty, I prefer to think through what I'm going to do and figure out the best way to do it. I imagine the impossible, dream big, and then try to figure out how the impossible can become the possible. After that, it's about how to turn the possible into reality.

Over the years, I've made it my business to study how things work and how people work—specifically, how things and people work best together to produce optimum results. That means creating an organization that can do great things and achieve more than any other organization can.

This book is about how to produce the best results as a real-world landscape contractor in the development, expansion, and *liberation* of your company. In the process, you will come to understand what the practice of landscaping—as a *business*—is, and what it isn't. If you keep focusing on what it isn't, you're destined for failure. But if you turn your sights on what it *is*, the tide will turn.

This book, intentionally small, is about big ideas. The topics we'll be discussing in this book are the very issues that landscape contractors face daily in their business. You know what they are: money, management, clients, and many more. My aim is to help you begin the exciting process of totally transforming the way you do business. As such, I'm confident that *The E-Myth Landscape Contractor* could well be the most important book on the practice of landscaping as a business that you'll ever read.

Unlike other books on the market, my goal is not to tell you how to do the work you do. Instead, I want to share with you the E-Myth philosophy as a way to revolutionize the way you think about the work you do. I'm convinced that this new way of thinking is something landscapers everywhere must adopt for their landscaping businesses to flourish during these trying times. I call it strategic thinking, as opposed to tactical thinking.

In strategic thinking, also called systems thinking, you, the landscaper, will begin to think about your entire company—the broad scope of it—instead of focusing on its individual parts. You will begin to see the end game (perhaps for the first time) rather than just the day-to-day routine that's consuming you—the endless, draining work I call "doing it, doing it, doing it."

Understanding strategic thinking will enable you to create a sole-proprietorship that becomes a successful business with the potential to flourish as an even more successful enterprise. But for you to accomplish this, your practice, your business, and certainly your enterprise must work *apart* from you instead of *because* of you.

The E-Myth philosophy defines a company as a sole proprietorship, a business, or an enterprise, so you will see these designations used throughout the book. In some industries, a company can also be called a practice or sole proprietorship. For the purposes of this book, my references to a "company" refer to a sole proprietorship.

Accordingly, a company is created and owned by a technician, a business is created and owned by a manager, and an enterprise is created and owned by an entrepreneur.

The E-Myth philosophy says that a highly successful landscaping company can grow into a highly successful landscaping business, which in turn can become the foundation for an inordinately successful landscaping enterprise that runs smoothly and efficiently *without* the landscape contractor having to be in the office for ten hours a day, six days a week.

So what is the E-Myth, exactly? The E-Myth is short for the Entrepreneurial Myth, which says that most businesses fail to fulfill their potential because most people starting their own businesses are not entrepreneurs at all. They're actually what I call *technicians suffering from an entrepreneurial seizure*. When technicians suffering from an entrepreneurial seizure start a landscaping company of their own, they almost always end up working themselves into a frenzy. Their days are booked solid with appointments, one client after another. These landscape contractors are burning the candle at both ends, fueled by too much coffee and too little sleep, and most of the time, they can't even stop to think.

In short, the E-Myth says that most landscapers don't own a true business—most own a job. They're doing it, doing it, doing it, hoping like hell to get some time off, but never figuring out how to get their business to run without them. And if your business doesn't run well without you, what happens when you can't be in two places at once? Ultimately, your business will fail.

There are a number of prestigious schools throughout the world dedicated to teaching the science of landscaping. The problem is they fail to teach the *business* of it. And because no one is being taught how to run a practice as a business, some landscape contractors find themselves having to close their doors every year. You could be a world-class expert in trees, native species, or building water features, but when it comes to building a successful business, all that specified knowledge matters exactly zilch.

The good news is you don't have to be among the statistics of failure in the landscaping profession. The E-Myth philosophy I am about to share with you in this book has been successfully applied to thousands of landscaping companies just like yours with extraordinary results.

The key to transforming your company—and your life—is to grasp the profound difference between going to work *on* your business (systems thinker) and going to work *in* your business (tactical thinker). In other words, it's the difference between going to work on your business as an entrepreneur and going to work in your business as a landscaper.

The two are not mutually exclusive. In fact, they are essential to each other. The problem with most landscaping companies is that the systems thinker—the entrepreneur—is completely absent. And so is the vision.

The E-Myth philosophy says that the key to transforming your company into a successful enterprise is to transform yourself from a successful landscape technician into a successful technician-manager-entrepreneur. In the process, everything you do in your landscaping business will be transformed. The door is then open to turning it into the kind of business it should be—a company, a business, an enterprise of pure joy.

The E-Myth not only *can* work for you, it *will* work for you. In the process, it will give you an entirely new experience of your business and beyond.

To your future and your life. Good reading.

—Michael E. Gerber
Co-Founder/Chairman
Michael E. Gerber Companies, Inc.
Carlsbad, California
www.michaelegerber.com/co-author

ACKNOWLEDGMENTS

Michael E. Gerber

As always, and never to be forgotten, there are those who give of themselves to make my work possible.

To my dearest and most forgiving partner, wife, friend, and co-founder, Luz Delia Gerber, whose love and commitment takes me to places I would often not go unaccompanied.

To Helen Chang, noble warrior, editor, brave soul, and sojourner, who covers all the bases we would have missed had she not been there.

To Erich Broesel, our stand-alone graphic designer and otherwise visual genius who supported the creation of all things visual that will forever be all things Gerber, we thank you, deeply, for your continuous contribution of things both temporal and eternal.

To Trish Beaulieu, wow, you are splendid.

And to Nancy Ratkiewich, whose work has been essential for you who are reading this.

To Johanna Nilsson, who told us that social media was much, much more than just social, and then, with the grace G-d gave her, proved it every step of the way.

To those many, many dreamers, thinkers, storytellers, and leaders, whose travels with me in The Dreaming Room have given me life, breath, and pleasure unanticipated before we met. To those many participants in my life (you know who you are), thank you for taking me seriously, and joining me in this exhilarating quest.

And, of course, to my co-authors, all of you, your genius, wisdom, intelligence, and wit have supplied me with a grand view of the world, which would never have been the same without you.

Love to all.

ACKNOWLEDGMENTS

Tony Bass

First, this story is not possible without the support and encouragement of my family.

To my wife, Lynn, forever strong and beautiful: You have given me these two amazing children, Holly and Maxx, who inspire me daily to continue to grow personally and professionally. Thanks to each of you and your help to keep my mornings quiet while I wrote this book.

To Dad. All those late nights in the shop provided a foundation of mechanics, creativity, and problem solving that stays with me daily. Thank you for taking the time to teach me.

To Mom. A fondness for a summer flower garden, a rose bush, and fresh vegetables from the garden introduced me to the landscape.

To Grandpa West, God rest his soul. Thanks for introducing me to the world of contracting and providing me the chance to experience my first job site.

To Grandpa Bass, rest in peace. Daily breakfast meetings in your late years created an urgency to place systems in the business. For this, I am forever grateful.

To Michael E. Gerber. Thanks for the inspiration and direction so many years ago with the *E-Myth*. Thanks for the challenge to now create *The E-Myth Landscape Contractor*.

To my clients around the world who have purchased Super Lawn Trucks™, *The Money Making Secrets of a Multi-Million Dollar Landscape Contractor*, Super Lawn Training programs, and Tony Bass' speaking services past and future: Thank you!

I love entrepreneurs! Entrepreneurs create their future. Come with me to create *your* future!

INTRODUCTION

Michael E. Gerber

A s I write this book, the recession may have ended, but it continues to take its toll on American businesses. Like any other industry, landscaping is not immune. Landscapers all over the country are watching as clients defer spending on their outside living spaces and business landscapes. At a time when per capita disposable income is at an all-time low, many people are choosing not to spend their hard-earned money on landscaping services for themselves or even for their businesses. As a result, landscaping moves from the realm of necessity to luxury, and regrettably, well-maintained landscapes become an expendable concern while industry revenue takes a sizable dip into the red.

Faced with a struggling economy and fewer and fewer clients, many landscape contractors I've met are asking themselves, "Why did I ever become a landscaper in the first place?"

And it isn't just a money problem. After thirty-five years of working with small businesses, many of them landscaping companies, I'm convinced that the dissatisfaction experienced by countless landscapers is not just about money. To be frank, the recession doesn't deserve all the blame, either. While the financial crisis our country is facing certainly hasn't made things any better, the problem started long before the economy tanked. Let's dig a little deeper. Let's go back to school.

Can you remember that far back? Whichever university or college of agriculture you attended, you probably had some great teachers who helped you become the fine landscaper you are. These schools excel at teaching the science of agriculture and landscaping; they'll teach you everything you need to know about plants, soil, and irrigation. But what they *don't* teach is the consummate skill set needed to be a successful landscaper, and they certainly don't teach what it takes to build a successful landscaping enterprise.

Obviously, something is seriously wrong. The education that landscape professionals receive in school doesn't go far enough, deep enough, broad enough. Colleges of agriculture don't teach you how to relate to the *enterprise* of landscaping or to the *business* of landscaping; they only teach you how to relate to the *practice* of landscaping. In other words, they merely teach you how to be an *effective* rather than a *successful* landscaper. Last time I checked, they weren't offering degrees in success.

That's why most landscape contractors are effective, but few are successful. Although a successful landscaper must be effective, an effective landscaper does not have to be—and in most cases isn't—successful.

An *effective* landscaper is capable of executing his or her duties with as much certainty and professionalism as possible.

A *successful* landscaper, on the other hand, works balanced hours, has little stress, enjoys rich and rewarding relationships with friends and family, and has an economic life that is diverse and fulfilling and shows a continuous return on investment.

A successful landscaper finds time and ways to give back to the community but at little cost to his or her sense of ease.

A successful landscaper is a leader, not simply someone who teaches clients how to improve their property values and protect their investments, but a sage; a rich person (in the broadest sense of the word); a strong father, mother, wife, or husband; a friend, teacher, mentor, and spiritually grounded human being; and a person who can see clearly into all aspects of what it means to lead a fulfilling life.

So let's go back to the original question. Why did you become a landscaper? Were you striving just to be an effective one, or did you dream about real and resounding success?

I don't know how you've answered that question in the past, but I am confident that once you understand the strategic thinking laid out in this book, you will answer it differently in the future.

If the ideas here are going to be of value to you, it's critical that you begin to look at yourself in a different, more productive way. I am suggesting you go beyond the mere technical aspects of your daily job as a landscaper and begin instead to think strategically about your landscaping business as both a business and an enterprise.

I often say that most companies don't work—the people who own them do. In other words, most landscaping companies are jobs for the landscape contractors who own them. Does this sound familiar? The landscaper, overcome by an entrepreneurial seizure, has started his or her own company, become his or her own boss, and now works for a lunatic!

The result: the landscape contractor is running out of time, patience, and ultimately money. Not to mention paying the worst price anyone can pay for the inability to understand what a true company is, what a true business is, and what a true enterprise is—the price of his or her life.

In this book I'm going to make the case for why you should think differently about what you do and why you do it. It isn't just the future of your landscaping company that hangs in the balance. It's the future of your life.

The E-Myth Landscape Contractor is an exciting departure from my other sole-authored books. In this book, Tony Bass, an E-Myth expert—a licensed landscaper who has successfully applied the E-Myth to the development of his landscaping company—shares his secrets about how he achieved extraordinary results using the E-Myth paradigm. In addition to the time-tested E-Myth strategies and systems I'll be sharing with you, you'll benefit from the wisdom, guidance, and practical tips provided by a legion of landscapers who've been in your shoes.

The problems that afflict landscaping companies today don't only exist in the field of landscaping; the same problems are confronting every organization of every size in every industry in every country in the world. *The E-Myth Landscape Contractor* is next in a new series of

E-Myth Expert books that serves as a launching pad for Michael E. Gerber Partners™ to bring a legacy of expertise to small, struggling businesses in *all* industries. This series offers an exciting opportunity to understand and apply the significance of E-Myth methodology in both theory and practice to businesses in need of development and growth.

The E-Myth says that only by conducting your business in a truly innovative and independent way will you ever realize the unmatched joy that comes from creating a truly independent business, a business that works *without* you rather than *because* of you.

The E-Myth says that it is only by learning the difference between the work of a *business* and the business of *work* that landscapers will be freed from the predictable and often overwhelming tyranny of the unprofitable, unproductive routine that consumes them on a daily basis.

The E-Myth says that what will make the ultimate difference between the success or failure of your landscaping company is first and foremost how you *think* about your business, as opposed to how hard you work in it.

So let's think it through together. Let's think about those things—work, clients, money, time—that dominate the world of landscapers everywhere.

Let's talk about planning. About growth. About management. About getting a life!

Let's think about improving your and your family's lives through the development of an extraordinary practice. About getting the life you've always dreamed of but never thought you could actually have.

Envision the future you want, and the future is yours.

The Story of Steve and Peggy

Michael E. Gerber

You leave home to seek your fortune and, when you get it, you go home and share it with your family.

—Anita Baker

Every business is a family business. To ignore this truth is to court disaster.

I don't care if family members actually work in the business or not. Whatever his or her relationship with the business, every member of a landscape contractor's family will be greatly affected by the decisions a landscape contractor makes about the business. There's just no way around it.

Unfortunately, like most businessmen, landscape contractors tend to compartmentalize their lives. They view their business as a profession—what they do—and therefore none of their family's business.

"This has nothing to do with you," says the landscape contractor to his wife, with blind conviction. "I leave work at the office and family at home."

And with equal conviction, I say, "Not true!"

In actuality, your family and landscaping company are inextricably linked to one another. What's happening in your company is also happening at home. Consider if each of the following is true:

- If you're angry at work, you're also angry at home.
- If you're out of control in your landscaping company, you're equally out of control at home.
- If you're having trouble with money in your company, you're also having trouble with money at home.
- If you have communication problems in your company, you're also having communication problems at home.
- If you don't trust in your company, you don't trust at home.
- If you're secretive in your company, you're equally secretive at home.

And you're paying a huge price for it!

The truth is that your company and your family are one—and you're the link. Or you should be. Because if you try to keep your company and your family apart, if your company and your family are strangers, you will effectively create two separate worlds that can never wholeheartedly serve each other. Two worlds that split each other apart.

Let me tell you the story of Steve and Peggy Walsh.

The Walshes met in college. They were lab partners in horticultural biology—Steve a student of landscape architecture and Peggy in floraculture. When their lab discussions started to wander beyond horticultural biology, plant physiology, and chemical analysis into their personal lives, they discovered they had a lot in common. By the end of the course, they weren't just talking in class, they were talking on the phone every night—and not about biology.

Steve thought Peggy was absolutely brilliant, and Peggy considered Steve the most passionate man she knew. It wasn't long before they were engaged and planning their future together. A week after graduation, they were married in a lovely garden ceremony outside Peggy's childhood home.

While Steve studied at a prestigious horticulture, landscape, and design college, Peggy attended a prestigious land-based college nearby. Over the next few years, the couple worked hard to keep their finances afloat. They worked long hours and studied constantly; they were often exhausted and struggled to make ends meet. But throughout it all, they were committed to what they were doing and to each other.

After passing the (C-27) Landscaping Contractor License Exam, Steve went on to get a master's degree in landscape architecture and environmental technologies, while Peggy completed her degree in floriculture and floristry operations and management. Then Steve started working for a large, multi-office landscaping company. Soon afterward, the couple had their first son, and Peggy decided to take some time off to be with him. Those were good years. Steve and Peggy loved each other very much, were active members in their church, participated in community organizations, and spent quality time together. The Walshes considered themselves one of the most fortunate families they knew.

But work became troublesome. Steve grew increasingly frustrated with the way the company was run. "I want to go into business for myself," he announced one night at the dinner table. "I want to start my own company."

Steve and Peggy spent many nights talking about the move. Was it something they could afford? Did Steve really have the skills necessary to make a landscaping company a success? Were there enough clients to go around? What impact would such a move have on Peggy's career managing a local plant nursery, their lifestyle, their son, their relationship? They asked all the questions they thought they needed to answer before Steve went into business for himself—but they never really drew up a concrete plan.

Finally, tired of talking and confident that he could handle whatever he might face, Steve committed to starting his own landscaping company. Because she loved and supported him, Peggy agreed, offering her own commitment to help in any way she could. So Steve quit his job, took out a second mortgage on their home, and leased a small office nearby.

In the beginning, things went well. A building boom had hit the town, and new families were pouring into the area. Steve had no trouble getting new clients. His company expanded, quickly outgrowing his office.

Within a year, Steve had employed an office manager, Clarissa, to book appointments and handle the administrative side of the business. He also hired a bookkeeper, Tim, to handle the finances. Steve was ecstatic with the progress his young company had made. He celebrated by taking his wife and son on vacation to Italy.

Of course, managing a business was more complicated and time-consuming than working for someone else. Steve not only supervised all the jobs Clarissa and Tim did, he was continually looking for work to keep everyone busy. When he wasn't scanning journals of landscaping and agriculture to stay abreast of what was going on in the field or fulfilling continuing-education requirements to stay current on the latest standards of turf management, horticulture, and irrigation, he was going to the bank, wading through client paperwork, or speaking with building management companies. He also found himself spending more and more time on the telephone dealing with client complaints and nurturing relationships.

As the months went by and more and more clients came through the door, Steve had to spend even more time just trying to keep his head above water.

By the end of its second year, the company, now employing two full-time and two part-time people, had moved to a larger office downtown. The demands on Steve's time had grown with the company.

He began leaving home earlier in the morning, returning home later at night. He drank more. He rarely saw his son anymore. For the most part, Steve was resigned to the problem. He saw the hard work as essential to building the "sweat equity" he had long heard about.

Money was also becoming a problem for Steve. Although the company was growing like crazy, money always seemed scarce when it was really needed. He had discovered that commercial property management companies were often slow to pay. He had to go through anywhere from two to three people before he could find someone to speak with about non-payment of invoices that were thirty, sixty, or even ninety days out.

When Steve worked for somebody else, he was paid twice a month. In his own company, he often had to wait—sometimes for months. He was still owed money on billings he had completed more than ninety days before.

When he complained to late-paying commercial property management companies, it fell on deaf ears. They would shrug, smile, and promise to do their best, adding, "But you know how business is. The real estate industry has taken a huge hit and we're lucky if we can collect thirty- to forty-five days out!"

Of course, no matter how slowly Steve got paid, he still had to pay his people. This became a relentless problem. Steve often felt like a juggler dancing on a tightrope. A fire burned in his stomach day and night.

To make matters worse, Steve began to feel that Peggy was insensitive to his troubles. Not that he often talked to his wife about the company. "Business is business" was Steve's mantra. "It's my responsibility to handle things at the office and Peggy's responsibility to take care of her own job and the family."

Peggy herself was working late hours at her job, and they'd brought in a nanny to help with their son. Steve couldn't help but notice that his wife seemed resentful, and her apparent lack of understanding baffled him. Didn't she see that he had a company to take care of? That he was doing it all for his family? Apparently not.

As time went on, Steve became even more consumed and frustrated by his company. When he went off on his own, he remembered saying, "I don't like people telling me what to do." But people were still telling him what to do. On one particularly frustrating morning, his office had to get authorization from the property manager before installing shrubs in front of a building. They spent twenty-five minutes on hold. Steve was furious.

Not surprisingly, Peggy grew more frustrated by her husband's lack of communication. She cut back on her own hours at the nursery to focus on their family, but her husband still never seemed to be around. Their relationship grew tense and strained. The rare moments they were together were more often than not peppered by long silences—a far cry from the heartfelt conversations that had characterized their relationship's early days, when they'd talk into the wee hours of the morning.

Meanwhile, Tim, the bookkeeper, was also becoming a problem for Steve. Tim never seemed to have the financial information Steve needed to make decisions about payroll, client billing, and general operating expenses, let alone how much money was available for Steve and Peggy's living expenses.

When questioned, Tim would shift his gaze to his feet and say, "Listen, Steve, I've got a lot more to do around here than you can imagine. It'll take a little more time. Just don't press me, okay?"

Overwhelmed by his own work, Steve usually backed off. The last thing Steve wanted was to upset Tim and have to do the books himself. He could also empathize with what Tim was going through, given the company's growth over the past year.

Late at night in his office, Steve would sometimes recall his first years out of school. He missed the simple life he and his family had shared. Then, as quickly as the thoughts came, they would vanish. He had work to do and no time for daydreaming. "Having my own company is a great thing," he would remind himself. "I simply have to apply myself, as I did in school, and get on with the job. I have to work as hard as I always have when something needs to get done."

Steve began to live most of his life inside his head. He began to distrust his people. They never seemed to work hard enough or to care about his company as much as he did. If he wanted to get something done, he usually had to do it himself.

Then one day, the office manager, Clarissa, quit in a huff, frustrated by the amount of work her boss was demanding of her. Steve was left with a desk full of papers and a telephone that wouldn't stop ringing.

Clueless about the work Clarissa had done, Steve was overwhelmed by having to pick up the pieces of a job he didn't understand. His world turned upside down. He felt like a stranger in his own company.

Why had he been such a fool? Why hadn't he taken the time to learn what Clarissa did in the office? Why had he waited until now?

Ever the trooper, Steve plowed into Clarissa's job with everything he could muster. What he found shocked him. Clarissa's workspace was a disaster area! Her desk drawers were a jumble of papers, coins, pens, pencils, rubber bands, envelopes, business cards, contact lenses, eye drops, and candy.

"What was she thinking?" Steve raged.

When he got home that night, even later than usual, he got into a shouting match with Peggy. He settled it by storming out of the house to get a drink. Didn't anybody understand him? Didn't anybody care what he was going through?

He returned home only when he was sure Peggy was asleep. He slept on the couch and left early in the morning, before anyone was awake. He was in no mood for questions or arguments.

When Steve got to his office the next morning, he immediately headed for the medicine cabinet. He had blisters on his hands, a backache, and a headache that just wouldn't quit! No matter how much pain he had physically, it was easier than having to deal with the mental anguish of his employee issues.

What lessons can we draw from Steve and Peggy's story? I've said it once and I'll say it again: *Every business is a family business.* Your business profoundly touches every member of your family, even if they never set foot inside your office. Every business either gives to the family or takes from the family, just as individual family members do.

If the business takes more than it gives, the family is always the first to pay the price.

In order for Steve to free himself from the prison he created, he would first have to admit his vulnerability. He would have to confess to himself and his family that he really didn't know enough about his own company and how to grow it.

Steve tried to do it all himself. Had he succeeded, had the company supported his family in the style he imagined, he would have burst with pride. Instead, Steve unwittingly isolated himself, thereby achieving the exact opposite of what he sought.

He destroyed his life—and his family's life along with it.

Repeat after me: *Every business is a family business.*

Are you like Steve? I believe that all landscape contractors share a common soul with him. You must learn that a business is only a business. It is not your life. But it is also true that your business can have a profoundly negative impact on your life unless you learn how to do it differently than most landscape contractors do it—and definitely differently than Steve did it.

Steve's landscaping company could have served his and his family's life. But for that to happen, he would have had to learn how to master his company in a way that was completely foreign to him.

Instead, Steve's company consumed him. Because he lacked a true understanding of the essential strategic thinking that would have allowed him to create something unique, Steve and his family were doomed from day one.

This book contains the secrets that Steve should have known. If you follow in Steve's footsteps, prepare to have your life and business fall apart. But if you apply the principles we'll discuss here, you can avoid a similar fate.

Let's start with the subject of *money*. But before we do, let's listen to the landscaper's view about the story I just told you. Let's talk about the story of Tony's career—and yours. ❧

CHAPTER

2

Stories of Landscapers – Past, Present, and Future

Tony Bass

A man should never neglect his family for business.

—Walt Disney

Ahuge crowd of people gathered at one of the Green Industry trade shows and educational training events. Landscapers, nurserymen, turfgrass professionals, arborists, and grounds maintenance companies were there to learn how to improve their businesses. They were walking the trade show floor to check out the latest equipment, new plant introductions, and business supplies to make their jobs better. They were also there to attend a few classes, obtain their pesticide applicators' continuing education credits, and learn the latest in industry research.

Future landscape professionals (horticulture students) were there also. Hundreds of these young people were walking the trade show floor. They moved in similarly-attired small groups, identifying with their schools by what color they all wore. They were from high schools, technical schools, and state universities. I was scheduled to give a short seminar to a group of these eager learners about "Careers in the Green Industry."

I was standing outside of the Super Lawn Trucks™ display booth and watching how the attendees responded to our display. I observed how my team would engage the people as they walked by and then entice them to enter the booth and admire our products. And I watched the attendees' body language during the walking tour around the Super Lawn Trucks™ models on display. Observe, think, and learn.

As I stood there, a familiar face appeared in the aisle with a group of students in tow. It was Jeff, a horticulture instructor at one of the technical colleges. He approached with an outstretched hand and a big smile, greeting me with an enthusiastic handshake. He stepped sideways and opened up his stance so his group of students would be included.

"Class, this is the man who I have told you about in my class. When I met Tony, he was wearing shorts, his knees were stained with red dirt, and I was helping to answer his horticulture questions back when I was the extension agent. And look at him today! He made a fortune with his landscaping business in a small community. He is dressed sharp, providing seminars, and promoting his truck business. You can learn a lot from Mr. Bass. This man is a good example of why you have made a good choice to study horticulture and landscaping."

I was a little surprised and humbled by his enthusiastic introduction. Of course, I smiled! Then I took the opportunity to address the small group. "Jeff helped me in the early days of my business and he is helping you learn the technical basics of landscaping today. If you will attend my seminar later today, I will share exactly what you have to do to be a business success with the technical skills you are now learning. There are incredible opportunities in the landscape industry! I'm glad that each of you is here!"

Jeff said, "We will be there, Tony. It's great to see you again! I always tell your story to my students."

Then, just as quickly, they moved on. Another familiar face appeared in the aisle. It was Johnny, yet another horticulture instructor at one of the state's technical colleges. Johnny smiled as he approached, but there were no students in tow.

Johnny stuck out his hand and said, "Tony, good to see you again. How are you?"

I replied, "Super, thanks for asking! Are you still teaching?"

"Oh, yes. I am still teaching. I have a couple of more years before I can retire. But enrollment is down, and with all the cuts in the state's education budget, I just hope the program continues until I can retire. We only had a dozen students last semester. And with all the challenges in the economy, I don't think there are a lot of jobs for them anyway."

"Really? Tell me more."

"Tony, you know how competitive this industry is. It's hard to make money in landscaping. In fact, I tell my students they might have a better chance of making money if they get into computers or something like that. Between the government regulations, the illegal immigrant labor problems, cutthroat pricing, and this economic slowdown, it's tough to make it in the landscape business. After all, that's why I closed my company and got the teaching job a few years ago."

"Wow! That is a very interesting story! I hope you and your students will attend my seminar later today."

"I didn't bring any students. I just came by to get a few pesticide applicator credits to keep my license current and walk the trade show floor. I'll be leaving for home soon."

I could not believe what had just happened to me. This was the perfect example, in real living color, of what happens in life and in business every single day. There are those who believe in scarcity and those who believe in abundance. And whatever you believe in, you're correct.

From whom would you rather learn: Jeff, the teacher who believes in abundance? Or Johnny, the teacher who believes in scarcity? Which story is closest to reality for the professional landscape contractor? Let's find out.

The Landscape Industry

First, let's look at the definition of landscaping services supplied by the US Census Bureau. The assigned numerical identification for the landscape industry is 561730. The North American Industry

Classification System (NAICS) is designed to help the government organize data for several thousand types of businesses. Here is the official definition:

561730 Landscaping Services

This industry comprises (1) establishments primarily engaged in providing landscape care and maintenance services and/or installing trees, shrubs, plants, lawns, or gardens and (2) establishments primarily engaged in providing these services along with the design of landscape plans and/or the construction (i.e., installation) of walkways, retaining walls, decks, fences, ponds, and similar structures.

How well does this definition describe your business? I bet you will agree it describes your business very well if you operate a landscaping company. Our government understands what we do, and our government has incredible resources to measure the key economic indicators of this industry. Let's take a look at the recent financial performance of this industry as reported by the US Census Bureau.

Figure 1

	# of US Employer Landscape Firms	Gross Receipts in Dollars	Annual Payroll In Dollars	# Paid Employees
2002	76,102	$35,171,624,000	$11,544,469,000	477,932
2007	93,687	$53,910,432,000	$17,388,531,000	596,896

Source: US Census Bureau Industry Statistics NAICS 561730

Over the five-year period between 2002 and 2007, which was an incredible period of economic expansion for the US, the data show an increase of 23 percent in the number of firms. Our industry added 17,585 landscaping companies. This translates into adding 3,517 new companies per year, or 9.63 new companies per day. Further, industry sales grew from $35 billion in revenue to nearly $54 billion—a whopping 53 percent growth! Landscape companies employed more than half a million workers nationwide by the year 2007. Please consider the message here. The number of firms grew by 23 percent while sales grew by 53 percent and the number of employees grew by just 24 percent.

The data show that this industry exploded in sales volume. We also see that companies learned how to increase sales over 50 percent without increasing the labor force by 50 percent. In other words, we dramatically increased productivity as an industry. How did your firm compare during this period of economic expansion?

Now let's look at how these industry numbers translate into individual company performance. How does your company compare to these key benchmark areas?

Figure 2

	Average Sales/ Firm	Average Number of Employees/Firm	Average Pay/ Employee	Average Sales/ Employee	Payroll as a % of Sales
2002	$ 462,164	6.3	$ 24,155	$ 73,591	32.82%
2007	$ 575,431	6.4	$ 29,132	$ 90,318	32.25%

Source: US Census Bureau Industry Statistics NAICS 561730

This data show the average landscape company has six or seven employees. The average employee is paid about one-third of the sales that employee generates. The great news is that landscape firm employees had a pay increase of just over 20 percent during the period, beating the inflation rate (11 percent) during that same period by 9 percent. In summary, the average employee working in this industry saw his pay increase 20 percent while the average company saw its sales increase almost 25 percent. The story is clear for this industry: growth, growth, growth.

Back to our story of the two teachers and what they were telling their young students. Is this an industry of abundance, ripe with opportunity? Or is this an industry of scarcity, with little potential? There are more data sets to examine before we reach a conclusion.

First, our government goes to great effort to collect data, segment that data, and use that data to improve our understanding of what we accomplish. It is important for you to know that the above data are incomplete. Please note from Figure 1, in the first column, the heading "# of US Employer Landscape Firms." Note the word *employer*. This figure refers only to companies who actually have employees. And as you will see below, there are many more data to consider.

Take a look at Figure 3, the data on *non-employer* firms.

Figure 3

	# of US Non-Employer Landscape Firms	Gross Receipts	Average Sales/Firm
2002	209,072	$ 4,811,183,000	$ 23,012
2007	312,456	$ 7,922,521,000	$ 25,356

Source: US Census Bureau Industry Statistics NAICS 561730

During the five-year period, the number of new non-employer firms exploded by a whopping 49.5 percent and sales grew 64 percent within non-employer companies in the landscape industry. However, the average sales per non-employer firm only grew 10 percent during this period, not even keeping pace with inflation (again, 11 percent) during that five-year period. The average non-employer firm *did not* increase their income.

Before those of you who operate one of the 94,000 employer firms with six to seven employees get bent out of shape about all of these small, start-up landscape firms, let's look a little closer at the data in Figure 4.

Figure 4

	Total Industry Sales	% Sales Employer Firms	% Sales Non-Employer Firms
2002	$ 39,982,807,000	88.0%	12.0%
2007	$ 61,832,953,000	87.2%	12.8%

Source: US Census Bureau Industry Statistics NAICS 561730

The data show that the non-employer firms produce a mere 12 percent of the sales in the industry although they outnumber employer firms 3.3 to 1. This collection of one-man armies, more than 300,000 firms, produces less in sales on average than one employee at an employer firm by a factor of 3.5 to 1.

Could it be that employer firms are more productive, or more likely is it that many of the non-employer firms are part-timers seeking supplemental income to their full-time jobs in some other field? My opinion is the latter.

However, it is quite clear from the recent data that the landscape industry has expanded and the consumer has many more service providers from which to choose. Have you felt the increase in competition inside your firm?

Let's talk about the 2008–2009 recession. During a period of 10 percent unemployment, do you think there were more people starting their own businesses? How about those landscape employees who were laid off during the recession? Did they find work in another industry, or did they follow the path Michael E. Gerber predicts?

Michael says businesses are not usually started by entrepreneurs but by "technicians suffering from an entrepreneurial seizure," the thesis for the E-Myth. Would a recession stimulate an increase in these "seizures"?

Both Michael and I believe that we are on a path to one of the greatest increases in self-employment and small business start-ups our society has ever witnessed. The unemployed, the under-employed, the "free agents," and the one-man armies need more money to survive. As expenses rise and the dollar buys less, starting a small business is one route many will take. Count on more competition.

Landscape Boom

Take a look at your client list today. Count the number of clients you serve who are over fifty years old. Is this the majority of your clients? If you don't know, find out. You need to know the demographics of those for whom you work.

It's possible that some seniors will downsize their homes. As they do this, expect smaller residential landscape projects to be the norm. Also expect to see more retirement communities. These seniors want to move away from the obligation of personal property maintenance. So expect to see more senior-citizen-focused homeowner associations.

As the aging population continues to grow, so does the landscape service industry. If you plan and prepare, your company can grow right along with it.

At certain times, the construction of new homes slows dramatically, as it did during the recession of 2008–2009. Landscape construction revenue and the average size of projects fell along with it. This was a big problem for construction-based firms. But let me give a few ways how, outside of new construction, the landscape industry can grow: The older you get, the more likely you will hire a lawn or landscape service.

- Age fifty and older is the largest demographic of consumers in the lawn and landscape market.
- Aging homes require more maintenance and repairs. Focus on the opportunity for the future.
- Gardening is America's number one hobby and this is unlikely to change, making landscaping a widely accepted area of home improvement.
- Environmental concerns, government mandates, and the "green" movement continue to create opportunities within the landscape industry.

- Plan, prepare, and position your firm to ride the wave of growth in backyard vegetable gardens, community gardens, and organic gardening. This part of the landscape industry began to explode during the recession. This trend will continue and create opportunities you never dreamed of.

Starting a lawn or landscaping company is not difficult and many more will come. As more companies offer services, more people buy services. So where does all this lead us? How can you think creatively about how to adapt your business to a changing market?

Grow Your Income

Face it. One prevalent thought in our society is that business ownership is a path toward wealth. This might be why you started your business. You wanted to earn more, be in control, and make your own future. I love you for your choice of entrepreneurship and the decision to join the landscape industry.

But what do you have to earn to be among the top income producers in the US? Let's look at the data in Figure 5 so you can benchmark your household income against our national averages.

Figure 5

Percentiles Ranked by AGI	AGI Threshold on Percentiles	Percentage of Federal Personal Income Tax Paid
Top 1%	$380,354	38.02
Top 5%	$159,619	58.72
Top 10%	$113,799	69.94
Top 25%	$ 67,280	86.34
Top 50%	$ 33,048	97.30
Bottom 50%	<$ 33,048	2.70

Note: AGI is Adjusted Gross Income
Source: Internal Revenue Service 2008

Take inventory of your own ability to produce income and compare it to the overall population of taxpayers in the US. When you submitted your last tax return, where did you fit on this chart? Are you in the 10 percent club according to our friends over at the IRS? Or are you in the bottom 50 percent that makes the top 50 percent possible?

Remember the statistics from Figure 2? The average pay for an employee at a landscape company was $29,132 in 2007. Please note that if you follow the averages, and you are one of those employees, you likely earn near the bottom 50 percent of taxpayers in the US. And unless you work for a company that is growing and creating management opportunities, which pay higher wages, you will likely stay at or near this income bracket for years to come. If your spouse works in your business or another, that adds to the household income, of course.

On the other hand, you might not be an employee but an employer or you are self-employed with no employees. You have a dream to join the top 1 percent if you are currently in the top 5 percent. Or you are in the top 50 percent and you have a dream to join the top 10 percent. It is human nature to seek improvement.

This takes us back to the question I posed earlier. Who is right: Jeff, who teaches abundance within the landscape industry, or Johnny, who warns students about scarcity?

The answer is clear to me: Jeff is right. Abundance is certainly possible. To achieve abundant income in the landscape industry, you have two choices:

1. Become an employer. Commit yourself to operating a company with employees. Recognize your firm must grow to become well above average.

2. Become an employee at a company that is on its way to become, or already is, well above average and requires a management team. From the data above, you now know what average is. Take this information to your company's owner and find out how your company compares. Do it right away if you seek abundance. Do not delay.

Conversely, Johnny is also right. You can certainly face scarcity of income while working in the landscape industry. Here's how you achieve this financial scarcity:

1. Become a one-man army, self-employed, non-employer lawn-service provider. It is highly unlikely you will join the 10 percent club of taxpayers in the US.

2. Become an employee at an average company with no plans for growth, expansion, or desire to develop the skills required to build an above-average company. Then just stick with this company and learn how to live on meager wages. Avoid the discussion of money and it will always be scarce in your life.

This book is not about the story of scarcity that Johnny teaches. This book is about the story that Jeff teaches. This book is about teaching you *my story* of how to achieve abundance as a landscape contractor. This is a story that passes well beyond being average or even above average. This book is about teaching you exactly what you have to do to build a world-class landscape company.

Some of you will read this chapter and say something like, "Tony only defines success in financial terms. How about the personal rewards of serving others, building beautiful landscapes, and caring for our environment?"

Don't worry. We will get to those things in later chapters.

I've worked in business for twenty-five years and no banker has ever asked me for a "personal satisfaction statement." The IRS doesn't ask for client lists or employee satisfaction surveys. The banks, the IRS, your accountant, and your family say one thing: "Show me the money!"

Personally, I have experienced both extremes of scarcity and abundance. The absence of money causes huge amounts of stress and strain. Then I have been blessed with an abundance of money. And this also causes stress and strain, but not in the same way.

Refer to Figure 5. How do you feel about the reality of joining the 10 percent club of taxpayers earning $113,799 per year and finding out that your exclusive fraternity pays 70 percent of all the taxes in the US?

According to the 2010 census, we have 308,745,538 people in the US. There were 139,960,580 tax returns filed in 2008. Numbers, numbers, numbers. People are counted. Money is counted, sorted, and organized into consistent formats. But a mere 13,996,058 of people, or 10 percent of the taxpayer population, paid 70 percent of our taxes. When you look at the data, the bottom 50 percent of taxpayers paid just 2.7 percent of our tax base.

Scarcity abounds in our society today. It is all around. But it doesn't have to be for you and your family. Choose to become an asset in the US balance sheet. Own your business and create jobs. Don't become a liability. Make money and pay your taxes.

To pay taxes and smile, you likely need a better understanding of money. You simply lack some basic money skills. You need more education about money. Let's call it *financial education*. And that's exactly what we will talk about in chapter 4.

This is a perfect time to hear what Michael has to teach us about money. ✤

CHAPTER

3

On the Subject
of Money

Michael E. Gerber

There are three faithful friends: an old wife, an old dog, and ready money.
—Benjamin Franklin

Had Steve and Peggy first considered the subject of money as we will here, their lives could have been radically different. Money is on the tip of every landscape contractor's tongue, on the edge (or at the very center) of every landscape contractor's thoughts, and intruding on every part of a landscape contractor's life.

With money consuming so much energy, why do so few landscape contractors handle it well? Why was Steve, like so many landscape contractors, willing to entrust his financial affairs to a relative stranger? Why is money scarce for most landscape contractors? Why is there less money than expected? And yet the demand for money is always greater than anticipated.

What is it about money that is so elusive, so complicated, so difficult to control? Why is it that every landscape contractor I've ever met hates to deal with the subject of money? Why are they almost always too late in facing money problems? And why are they constantly obsessed with the desire for more of it?

Money—you can't live with it and you can't live without it. But you better understand it and get your people to understand it. Because until you do, money problems will eat your business for lunch.

You don't need an accountant or financial planner to do this. You simply need to prod your people to relate to money very personally. From the maintenance novice to receptionist, they should all understand the financial impact of what they do every day in relationship to the company's profit and loss.

And so you must teach your people to think like owners, not like technicians or office managers or receptionists. You must teach them to operate like personal profit centers, with a sense of how their work fits in with the company as a whole.

You must involve everyone in the company with the topic of money—how it works, where it goes, how much is left, and how much everybody gets at the end of the day. You also must teach them about the four kinds of money the company creates.

The Four Kinds of Money

In the context of owning, operating, developing, and exiting from a landscape company, money can be split into four distinct but highly integrated categories:

- Income
- Profit
- Flow
- Equity

Failure to distinguish how the four kinds of money play out in your company is a surefire recipe for disaster.

Important Note: Do not talk to your accountants or bookkeepers about what follows; it will only confuse them and you. This information comes from the real-life experiences of thousands of small-business owners, landscapers included, most of whom were hopelessly confused about money when I met them. Once they understood and accepted the following principles, they developed clarity about money that could only be called enlightenment.

The First Kind of Money: Income

Income is the money a company pays its landscape contractors for doing their job *in* the company. It's what they get paid for going to work every day.

Clearly, if landscapers didn't do their job, others would have to, and they would be paid the money the company currently pays the landscapers. Income, then, has nothing to do with *ownership*. Income is solely the province of *employee-ship*.

That's why to the landscaper-*as-employee*, income is the most important form money can take. To the landscaper-as-*owner*, however, it is the least important form money can take.

Most important; least important. Do you see the conflict between the landscaper-as-employee and the landscaper-as-owner?

We'll deal with this conflict later. For now, just know that it is potentially the most paralyzing conflict in a landscape contractor's life.

Failing to resolve this conflict will cripple you. Resolving it will set you free.

The Second Kind of Money: Profit

Profit is what's left over after a landscaping company has done its job effectively and efficiently. If there is no profit, the company is doing something wrong.

However, just because the company shows a profit does not mean it is necessarily doing all the right things in the right way. Instead, it just means that something was done right during or preceding the period in which the profit was earned.

The important issue here is whether the profit was intentional or accidental. If it happened by accident (which most profit does), don't take credit for it. You'll live to regret your impertinence.

If it happened intentionally, take all the credit you want. You've earned it. Because profit created intentionally, rather than by accident, is replicable—again and again. And your company's ability to repeat its performance is the most critical ability it can have.

As you'll soon see, the value of money is a function of your company's ability to produce it in predictable amounts at an above-average return on investment.

Profit can be understood only in the context of your company's purpose, as opposed to *your* purpose as a landscape contractor. Profit, then, fuels the forward motion of the company that produces it. This is accomplished in four ways:

- Profit is *investment capital* that feeds and supports growth.
- Profit is *bonus capital* that rewards people for exceptional work.
- Profit is *operating capital* that shores up money shortfalls.
- Profit is *return-on-investment capital* that rewards you, the owner-operator, for taking risks.

Without profit, a landscaping company cannot subsist, much less grow. Profit is the fuel of progress.

If a company misuses or abuses profit, however, the penalty is much like having no profit at all. Imagine the plight of a landscape contractor who has way too much return-on-investment capital and not enough investment capital, bonus capital, and operating capital. Can you see the imbalance this creates?

The Third Kind of Money: Flow

Flow is what money *does* in a landscaping company, as opposed to what money *is*. Whether the company is large or small, money tends to move erratically through it, much like a pinball. One minute it's there; the next minute it's not.

Flow can be even more critical to a company's survival than profit, because a company can produce a profit and still be short of money. Has this ever happened to you? It's called profit on paper rather than in fact.

No matter how large your company, if the money isn't there when it's needed, you're threatened—regardless of how much profit you've made. You can borrow it, of course. But money acquired in dire circumstances is almost always the most expensive kind of money you can get.

Knowing where the money is and where it will be when you need it is a critically important task for both the landscaper-as-employee and the landscaper-as-owner.

Rules of Flow

You will learn no lesson more important than the huge impact flow can have on the health and survival of your landscaping company, let alone your business or enterprise. The following two rules will help you understand why this subject is so critical.

1. **The First Rule of Flow states that your income statement is static, while the flow is dynamic.** Your income statement is a snapshot, while the flow is a moving picture. So, while your income statement is an excellent tool for analyzing your company after the fact, it's a poor tool for managing it in the heat of the moment.

Your income statement tells you (1) how much money you're spending and where, and (2) how much money you're receiving and from where.

Flow gives you the same information as the income statement, plus it tells you when you're spending and receiving money. In other words, flow is an income statement moving through time. And that is the key to understanding flow. It is about management in real time. How much is coming in? How much is going out? You'd like to know this daily, or even by the hour if possible. Never by the week or month.

You must be able to forecast flow. You must have a flow plan that helps you gain a clear vision of the money that's out there next month and the month after that. You must also pinpoint what your needs will be in the future.

Ultimately, however, when it comes to flow, the action is always in the moment. It's about *now*. The minute you start to meander away from the present, you'll miss the boat.

Unfortunately, few landscape contractors pay any attention to flow until it dries up completely and slow pay becomes no pay. They are oblivious to this kind of detail until, say, clients announce that they won't pay for this or that. That gets a landscape contractor's attention because the expenses keep on coming.

When it comes to flow, most landscape contractors are flying by the proverbial seat of their pants. No matter how many people you hire to take care of your money, until you change the way you think about it, you will always be out of luck. No one can do this for you.

Managing flow takes attention to detail. But when flow is managed, your life takes on an incredible sheen. You're swimming with the current, not against it. You're in charge!

2. **The Second Rule of Flow states that money seldom moves as you expect it to.** But you do have the power to change that, provided you understand the two primary sources of money as it comes in and goes out of your landscaping business.

The truth is, the more control you have over the source of money, the more control you have over its flow. The sources of money are both inside and outside your company.

Money comes from *outside* your company in the form of receivables, reimbursements, investments, and loans.

Money comes from *inside* your company in the form of payables, taxes, capital investments, and payroll. These are the costs associated with attracting clients, delivering your services, handling operations, and so forth.

Few landscape contractors see the money going *out* of their company as a source of money, but it is.

When considering how to spend money in your business, you can save—and therefore make—money in three ways:

- Do it more effectively.
- Do it more efficiently.
- Stop doing it altogether.

By identifying the money sources inside and outside of your company, and then applying these methods, you will be immeasurably better at controlling the flow in your company.

But what are these sources? They include how you

- manage your services;
- buy supplies and equipment;
- compensate your people;
- plan people's use of time;
- determine the direct cost of your services;
- increase the number of clients seen;
- manage your work;
- collect account receivables; and
- countless more.

In fact, every task performed in your company (and ones you haven't yet learned how to perform) can be done more efficiently and effectively, dramatically reducing the cost of doing business. In the process, you will create more income, produce more profit, and balance the flow.

The Fourth Kind of Money: Equity

Sadly, few landscape contractors fully appreciate the value of equity in their landscaping company. Yet equity is the second most valuable asset any will ever possess. (The first most valuable asset is, of course, your life. More on that later.)

Equity is the financial value a prospective buyer places on your company.

Thus, your *company* is your most important product, not your services, because your company has the power to set you free. That's right. Once you sell your company—providing you get what you want for it—you're free!

Of course, to enhance your equity—to increase your value—you have to build it right. You have to build a company that works. A company that can become a true business, and a business that can become a true enterprise. A company/business/enterprise that can produce income, profit, flow, and equity better than any other landscape contractor's company can.

To accomplish that, your company must be designed so it can do what it does systematically and predictably, every single time.

The Story of McDonald's

Let me tell you what is probably the most unlikely story anyone has ever told you about the successful building of a landscaping company, business, and enterprise. Let me tell you the story of Ray Kroc.

You might be thinking, *What on earth does a hamburger stand have to do with my company? I'm not in the hamburger business; I'm a landscape contractor.*

Yes, you are. But by practicing landscaping as you have been taught, you've abandoned any chance to expand your reach, help more clients, or improve your services the way they must be improved if the business of landscaping—and your life—is going to be transformed.

The answer lies in Ray Kroc's story.

Kroc called his first McDonald's restaurant "a little money machine." That's why thousands of franchises bought it. And the reason it worked? Kroc demanded consistency, so that a hamburger in Philadelphia would be an advertisement for one in Peoria. In fact, no matter where you bought a McDonald's hamburger in the 1950s, the meat patty was guaranteed to weigh exactly 1.6 ounces, with a diameter of 3 ⅝ inches. It was in the McDonald's handbook.

Did Kroc succeed? You know he did! And so can you, once you understand his methods. Consider just one part of his story.

In 1954, Kroc made his living selling the five-spindle Multimixer milkshake machine. He heard about a hamburger stand in San Bernardino, California, that had eight of his machines in operation, meaning it could make forty shakes simultaneously. This he had to see.

Kroc flew from Chicago to Los Angeles, then drove sixty miles to San Bernardino. As he sat in his car outside Mac and Dick McDonald's restaurant, he watched as lunch customers lined up for bags of hamburgers.

In a revealing moment, Kroc approached a strawberry blonde in a yellow convertible. As he later described it, "It was not her sex appeal but the obvious relish with which she devoured the hamburger that made my pulse begin to hammer with excitement."

Passion.

In fact, it was the french fry that truly captured his heart. Before the 1950s, it was almost impossible to buy fries of consistent quality. Kroc changed all that. "The French fry," he once wrote, "would become almost sacrosanct for me, its preparation a ritual to be followed religiously."

Passion and preparation.

The potatoes had to be just so—top-quality Idaho russets, eight ounces apiece, deep-fried to a golden brown, and salted with a shaker that, as Kroc put it, kept going "like a Salvation Army girl's tambourine."

As Kroc soon learned, potatoes too high in water content—even top-quality Idaho russets varied greatly in water content—will come out soggy when fried. And so Kroc sent out teams of workers, armed with hydrometers, to make sure all his suppliers were producing potatoes in the optimal solids range of 20 to 23 percent.

Preparation and passion. Passion and preparation. Look those words up in the dictionary and you'll see Kroc's picture. Can you envision your picture there?

Do you understand what Kroc did? Do you see why he was able to sell thousands of franchises? Kroc knew the true value of equity, and, unlike Steve from our story, Kroc went to work *on* his business rather than *in* his business. He knew the hamburger wasn't his product—McDonald's was!

So what does *your* landscaping company need to do to become a little money machine? What is the passion that will drive you to build a company that works—a turnkey system like Ray Kroc's?

Equity and the Turnkey System

What's a turnkey system? And why is it so valuable to you? To better understand it, let's look at another example of a turnkey system that worked to perfection: the recordings of Frank Sinatra.

Sinatra's records were to him as McDonald's restaurants were to Ray Kroc. They were part of a turnkey system that allowed Sinatra to sing to millions of people without having to be present.

Sinatra's recordings were a dependable turnkey system that worked predictably, systematically, automatically, and effortlessly to produce the same results every single time—no matter where they were played, and no matter who was listening.

Regardless of where Sinatra was, his records just kept on producing income, profit, flow, and equity, over and over—and still do! Sinatra needed only to produce the prototype recording and the system did the rest.

Kroc's McDonald's is another prototypical turnkey solution, addressing everything McDonald's needs to do in a basic, systematic way so that anyone properly trained by McDonald's can successfully reproduce the same results.

And this is where you'll realize your equity opportunity: in the way your company does business; in the way your company systematically does what you intend it to do; and in the development of your turnkey system—a system that works even in the hands of ordinary people (and landscape contractors less experienced than you) to produce extraordinary results.

Remember:

- If you want to build vast equity in your company, then go to work *on* your company, building it into a business that works every single time.
- Go to work *on* your company to build a totally integrated turnkey system that delivers exactly what you promised every single time.
- Go to work *on* your company to package it and make it stand out from the landscaping companies you see everywhere else.

Here is the most important idea you will ever hear about your company and what it can potentially provide for you:

The value of your equity is directly proportional to how well your company works. And how well your company works is directly proportional to the effectiveness of the systems you have put into place upon which the operation of your company depends.

Whether money takes the form of income, profit, flow, or equity, the amount of it—and how much of it stays with you—invariably boils down to this. Money, happiness, life—it all depends on how well your company works. Not on your people, not on you, but on the system.

Your company holds the secret to more money. Are you ready to learn how to find it?

Earlier in this chapter, I alerted you to the inevitable conflict between the landscaper-as-employee and the landscaper-as-owner. It's a battle between the part of you working in the company and the part of you working on the company. Between the part of you working for income and the part of you working for equity.

Here's how to resolve this conflict:

- Be honest with yourself about whether you're filling employee shoes or *owner* shoes.
- As your company's key employee, determine the most effective way to do the job you're doing, *and then document that job.*
- Once you've documented the job, create a strategy for replacing yourself with someone else (another landscape

contractor, or, even better, a technician) who will then use your documented system exactly as you do.

- Have your new employees manage the newly delegated system. Improve the system by quantifying its effectiveness over time.

- Repeat this process throughout your company wherever you catch yourself acting as employee rather than owner.

- Learn to distinguish between ownership work and employee-ship work every step of the way.

Master these methods, understand the difference between the four kinds of money, develop an interest in how money works in your company—and then watch it flow in with the speed and efficiency of an avalanche.

Now let's take another step in our strategic thinking process. Let's look at the subject of *planning*. But first, let's listen to what Tony has to say about money. ✤

CHAPTER 4

Where Is My Money?

Tony Bass

Money is in some respects life's fire: it is a very excellent servant, but a terrible master.

—P.T. Barnum

Money confuses people, especially landscape contractors. I will admit that money confused me for years. If you have ever been confused by the lack of money in your business or personal life, you are in the majority. If you have ever been confused by having too much money in your life, you are in the minority. However, both situations can be equally confusing. I have faced each situation in my career.

In the early days of my career, there was never enough money. But after building a real business, with real profits, solid client contracts, and dependable cash flow, money was no longer the elusive creature that I craved, hunted, and then watched quickly disappear.

Money became an important tool for my landscape business. The very first type of money I sought in my business was profit. *Profit* was a really cool word. I was forced to learn the definition of profit in an accounting class in college. The equation was pretty simple.

Sales – Expenses = Profit

The Redheaded Accountant

I hired an accountant to help me keep track of my money the very first year in business. A nice lady, she was tall, thin, nicely dressed, and always professional. She was the person who could help me keep track of all the money that would be coming in. She came highly recommended.

Each month, I would dutifully visit her office, turn in my check stubs, bank statement, invoices, receipts, and relevant financial records. In return, she would provide me with a financial report a few weeks later. I would occasionally sit with her and ask questions about this financial report. This financial report she produced was not as easy to understand as the equation above. It didn't look like the simple formula I remembered from accounting class.

First, there was the income statement. There was a line labeled *sales.* There was a line labeled *expenses.* And, yes, there was a line labeled *profit.* But there was an obvious problem with her accounting. The profit never equaled what was in my checking account. I began to wonder, *Is my accountant a liar and a cheater?*

She would give me a report telling me I had profit. But in my checking account, there was nowhere near that amount of money. I knew I hadn't taken it out of my checking account, so where was the money?

"It's in the balance sheet," she would often say. "You know that pickup truck you bought? You paid cash for it, right? A lot of your profit has been used to buy that truck. Here is the lawn mower, the string trimmer, a blower, and other tools. Now, you can find all that money right here on the balance sheet."

"Oh," I said. "I get it. It's in the balance sheet."

Then she spoke the most confusing words I had heard up till that winter day. She said, "You owe $7,000 to the IRS for your federal income taxes by April 15."

"Wait a minute," I said. "I don't have $7,000 in my checking account."

The accountant said, "Well, that's what you owe. You still have a couple of months before it is due. So you need to get ready to pay it."

Talk about being confused about money. This young man was confused! Where in the world would I find $7,000 to pay taxes in sixty days? The government was about to get rich off of my business and me. I decided I'd better get to work. I needed to make some more money.

I got back to work, sold some jobs, worked my butt off six days a week, and just in time for April 15, I paid that $7,000 tax bill. What a relief. *Now I can finally make some money for me,* I thought.

The new business opportunities continued. As I took on more jobs, I needed more equipment to serve more clients. And if I needed it, I bought it. After all, I wanted a lot of money. I wanted a lot of profit. So I would surely need a lot of customers.

As my checking account grew over the next few months, I knew I was making money. Busy, busy, busy. Spring, summer, and fall were very busy times. I didn't have as much free time to sit with the accountant.

After all, it was sort of awkward going into the accountant's office—it was so clean. When I would go by there, it was between jobs, and I was so—dirty. She was dressed nicely in her suit; I was in my shorts. My knees were blackened by the stains from a sodding job; her knees were covered by pantyhose. So I tried not to stay long. Just dropped off my stuff and left quickly.

As the year ended, winter came and work slowed down so I finally had some time to meet with the accountant. I planned a day where I could meet with her in the morning—while I was still clean—and we could review the financial statements. I wanted to talk about this "tax thing" she'd hit me with the previous year. I didn't want any surprises this time.

This was my second full year of business and I had posted another small profit. It was more money than I made in my part-time grocery store job in college, so I was satisfied that I was making progress in my quest for "a lot of money" as a businessman. But one thing was clear:

My friends who took jobs after college were making more money than I was. I knew this because they bragged about their salaries.

I sat down with my accountant to discuss the financial statements she had prepared.

And the same damned thing happened again! According to her, I had made some profit. My sales had nearly doubled, but my profit was smaller. I only owed $5,000 in taxes this year.

I said to my accountant, "You have got to be kidding! I doubled my sales and I made less profit? How can that happen?"

She said, "Looking over your income statement, it looks like your labor expenses grew a lot this year. Did you hire some new people?"

I responded, "I had to hire a couple of guys to help me get it all done. In fact, these guys are so good; they taught me a few things about landscaping this year. They had prior experience, and after all, I couldn't do that much in sales by myself. I am lucky to have such good guys working with me. I am going to keep these guys. We can kick some landscaping butt. You should come see some of our projects."

So I asked my accountant, "Do you have any suggestions on how I can keep from having a huge tax bill each year? I mean, it's hard to come up with thousands of dollars to pay taxes just as winter is ending."

The accountant said, "Well, Tony, many of my small business owner clients pay themselves a regular salary and withhold payroll taxes on themselves just like you are doing on your employees. You don't really pay less money in taxes that way, but you will pay your tax bill each pay period of the month."

I said, "A salary? I turned down the grocery store job because I don't want a salary. I want some big profits from my business! Now every time I make some profits, you make me pay a bunch of taxes. Are you telling me everything I need to know about business records, money, and taxes? I really feel like you are holding back information on me. Please explain to me what you are holding back. Do you work for me or the IRS?"

Talk about being confused. I was confused. And apparently, based on the reaction I got from my accountant, I was confusing her too.

She said, "Look, I am a CPA, which stands for Certified Public Accountant. I have a sworn responsibility to properly inform you on how to comply with financial recordkeeping and tax reporting or I can lose my CPA license. I am trying to keep you from violating any tax laws, for crying out loud!"

"Listen up, Tony," she continued. "I suggest that you begin taking a regular salary check. Take it each week when you pay your guys, withhold the payroll taxes based on your gross salary, and recognize the deductions based on your W-4 form, just like I have taught you to do for your employees. This way you won't have a huge tax bill at the end of each year. Or just keep doing what you've been doing and you will face a big tax payment. It's your choice!"

I told my accountant, "I don't really need a salary. I don't have many personal expenses. In fact, I would rather reinvest my profits into my growing my business. Let me think about this salary thing."

After all, it was winter again. Work had slowed down. I had these great guys I had to keep busy. I had a $5,000 tax bill to pay. It would be difficult to begin taking a salary over the winter.

And then with a suspicious reluctance, after paying the $5,000 tax bill, I began to implement the new company policy of taking a regular salary paycheck from my business. I have to admit, having a regular paycheck—a set amount of money to call my own—was a satisfying feeling.

My personal bank account began to grow with this new salary strategy. After all, at the time I was young, living with my mom and dad, and I didn't have many personal expenses. I needed funds for my monthly college loan payment, gas money, some weekend travel expenses, and a few bucks to take out a really cute girlfriend on dates. I didn't need a big salary like my friends with regular jobs. Just a little salary would do.

I thought, *This time next year, I have got it all figured out. I will not have a huge tax bill to pay at the end of the winter. I will take a salary, and I will make me some personal money.*

At the same time, I was ready for big growth. *I will add another crew this year. I am going to try to double sales again. I can finally make some really big money! Salary and profits!*

Apparently, something went wrong. Really wrong. Although we continued to grow sales, profit seemed to be non-existent. No matter how much money I deposited into the bank each month, it was never enough to meet all my obligations. I was working in the field six days a week, every week. No time for dating or weekend ballgames. Heck, I even gave up hunting season. I spent Sundays drawing landscape plans, writing estimates, and doing paperwork that could not be done during the busy weekdays while the crews were there.

I continued to visit the accountant each month and provide the documents she requested to organize my financial reports. But no matter what I provided, the information she gave me in return was more confusing than ever. Sales were growing—that much was clear. But what was happening to my bottom line?

Where were the profits? Why did the profits not grow as well as sales? What was happening? How could this be happening? Where were the profits?

When I sat with the accountant, I asked her these exact questions. The only thing she offered was this: "Tony, your expenses are growing equal to or greater than your new sales. There is no more profit. Unless you have forgotten to give me some deposits, the reports are correct. Could you be missing some deposits? Have you billed all your clients for all your work properly?"

As the accountant asked me these questions, the light bulb went off in my head.

I said to the accountant, "You know, with all the growth in sales, I have been super busy getting the work done in the field. I have fallen behind on getting the invoices sent out. There are two or three landscaping jobs that we have completed but have yet to be billed out or collected.

"And now that you mention it, I did not get my monthly maintenance contracts billed out before last month ended. I usually send those out the last week of the month, but I just got behind trying to finish up a big project."

And then this nicely dressed, perfumed, tall, slender, and redheaded accountant said the most confusing thing. She said, "Tony, your cash flow is not going to be good if you don't invoice your clients on time each month. You really need to find time to bill out your jobs promptly as you finish them. And here is another suggestion, Tony. Make sure you collect the money you bill as quickly as possible. With growth like you are experiencing, cash flow is going to be important to manage each and every month!"

"Cash flow? Can you please explain cash flow?" I asked.

The accountant explained, "Cash flow is the speed and volume of money as it moves through your company. The faster you can get a job completed, billed out, and the money deposited in the bank, the better cash flow will be.

"Basically, you are running short on cash because you are doing work, paying for materials, paying your labor, and paying for the cost of equipment in advance of getting paid for the jobs. So you are using money from credit cards, vendor trade accounts, and your equity to finance operations.

"Your cash flow would definitely improve if you would get your jobs billed out faster and the money collected more promptly. In fact, let's take a look at this statement of cash flows from the accounting software we use for your financial reports. I can show you what I mean."

We took a few minutes and looked over this statement of cash flows. This was a report I had never seen in the past three-plus years of running my landscape business. I felt like I understood what she showed me as she explained each line of numbers. But as I sat there, an Elvis Presley song called "Suspicious Minds" popped into my mind.

I now had clear evidence. My accountant had been withholding critical information. We had never discussed cash flow. Just as I had suspected the previous year, she was not telling me everything I needed to know. At that instant I made a decision: My accountant was a liar and a cheat. It had just taken me three years to finally catch her. She was not telling me what I really needed to know. *She must be working for the IRS. She sure isn't working for me.*

I began to look at my accountant with complete distrust. I thought, *I will have to find another accountant! I will find me an accountant who will be honest with me and who will teach me what I need to* know in advance. I want an accountant who can help me solve my money problems and who will not withhold critical information.

So after that meeting, I began to search for a new accountant.

Does this story sound familiar to you? Has there been a time in your business career that you felt like your accountant was with-holding information? Have you ever felt like your accountant was not giving you all the answers? Have you ever felt like the financial statements were just too confusing to completely understand? I know you probably have felt this way. You might have these same kinds of questions.

Your Money Plan

As I write this story, I have worked with more than two hundred owners of privately held landscaping companies. Fewer than twenty of these company owners could provide me a copy of up-to-date financial statements and explain the story revealed within those financial statements. I have met even fewer who can use their financial statements and compare their financial statistics to similar-sized, successful companies in the landscape industry. In other words, my experience has demonstrated that only about 10 percent of the owners of landscaping companies understand money inside their business.

If you happen to be in the 10 percent who can produce, under-stand, explain, and compare your financial history with the most successful landscaping firms in the industry, congratulations! You have developed one of the skills necessary to operate a successful, consistently profitable firm. However, this skill does not guarantee that you will always operate a profitable firm.

It is amazing, really. Michael E. Gerber was the very first person who shared that sobering statistic on small business failure. I read these words in the fifth year of my company. As I read these words in *The E-Myth: Why Most Business Don't Work and What To Do About It*, a huge knot began to develop in my gut:

"Businesses start and fail in the United States at an increasingly staggering rate. Every year, more than 500,000 people start a business of some sort. By the end of the first year, at least 40 percent of them will be out of business. Within five years, more than 80 percent of them – 400,000 – will have failed."

A swelling fear developed inside me that my company would become another statistic for failed businesses. I was in my fifth year of business—and I had just learned there was an 80 percent chance I wouldn't make it. No wonder that accountant didn't tell me everything I needed to know about money. She probably didn't think I would make it either!

Shortly after reading *The E-Myth* and taking my six-month sabbatical to reinvent my business, I built my first written business plan. This business plan included a projection of revenue, direct job costs, overhead, and planned profits for my firm.

I took this business plan into three local banks. It was a neatly bound report with a clearly stated purpose. I was asking for a business expansion loan. I was seeking money.

Amazingly, one banker quickly said, "This isn't the kind of business we work with."

It was a kind way to say no to my loan request.

The second banker said, "I will read your plan. We might be interested in this type of business."

The third banker said, "It looks like you have put a lot of effort into your plan. I will read it and take it to the loan committee for consideration."

I followed up with the two bankers for the next thirty days. I had a few questions I needed to answer about my twenty-five-page business plan. But mostly, my phone calls were about asking if I had been approved.

Every banker said, "I'm still working on it."

I asked, "What can I do to help you make a decision to grant me this loan?"

And then one cold winter day, I heard these magic words from one banker: "Tony, you are approved!"

There was no co-signer needed. (Dad would be relieved.) I just needed to come by, sign the papers, and pick up my check. It was like the floodgates of money had been opened, and I was drowning in money. I had more money in my checking account than ever before.

As I left the bank that day, I had a nervous feeling: *What if my plans are wrong and I can't repay this loan?* I admit having a pile of money in my account made me nervous. But I pressed onward to execute my business expansion plan.

Until I sat down, thought about where I wanted my business to go, and wrote my goals on paper, money was always elusive and hard to get. But when Michael E. Gerber explained to me how I must work *on* the business instead of working *in* the business, I began to understand and look for the different types of money in my own company.

As it turned out, the redheaded accountant was not a liar and a cheat after all. I simply did not have enough financial education or business experience to know what questions to ask about money. When you think about it, she had signed on to be the financial historian. She had no idea where my future business was going or where my future money might come from. How could she know where my business was going? I had never told her.

For that matter, I didn't even know where my business was going. I had never laid out a financial plan of where I wanted to go in the future.

Ask your accountant about future sales, future income, future cash flow, or future equity and she will get a funny look on her face. If you have been looking for financial answers about your financial future from your accountant, and you are having trouble, you are not alone. Have you ever heard this famous line from the movie *Cool Hand Luke*: "What we've got here is failure to communicate"?

The well-written business plan I created focused on the future. This business plan became a communication tool within my business. I focused on communicating how we could improve the operational processes and procedures within my firm. What I had learned over my six-month sabbatical studying, investigating, testing, and simply thinking of how we could improve the largest part of my company, our daily operations, led me to an epiphany.

Money would not stay in my company unless we had dependable, flawless, operational systems. That's what Michael E. Gerber had explained in *The E-Myth*.

And there was this new issue regarding money. I had once heard this word in past discussions with the redheaded, sweet-smelling accountant. The word was *equity*. And Michael E. Gerber said this was the most important kind of money.

So I used that *equity* word in a small portion of the written business plan. I was on my way to get me some of that new kind of money: equity. I would no longer be satisfied with profits, salary, and cash flow. From that day forward, I wanted me some equity!

Read on to see what Michael has to say about planning. ✤

CHAPTER

5

On the Subject of Planning

Michael E. Gerber

Luck is good planning, carefully executed.

—Anonymous

A nother obvious oversight revealed in Steve and Peggy's story was the absence of true planning.

Every landscaper starting his or her own company must have a plan. You should never begin to see clients without a plan in place. But, like Steve, most landscape contractors do exactly that. Start without a plan.

A landscape contractor lacking a plan is simply someone who goes to work every day. Someone who is just doing it, doing it, doing it. Busy, busy, busy. Maybe making money, maybe not. Maybe getting something out of life, maybe not. Taking chances without really taking control.

The plan tells anyone who needs to know *how we do things here.* The plan defines the objective and the process by which you will

45

attain it. The plan encourages you to organize tasks into functions, and then helps people grasp the logic of each of those functions. This in turn permits you to bring new employees up to speed quickly.

There are numerous books and seminars on the subject of business management, but they focus on making you a better landscaper. I want to teach you something that you've never been taught before: how to be a manager. It has nothing to do with conventional business management and everything to do with thinking like an entrepreneur.

The Planning Triangle

As we discussed in the preface, every landscaping sole proprietorship is a company, every landscaping business is a company, and every landscaping enterprise is a company. Yet the difference between the three is extraordinary. Although all three may offer landscaping services, how they do what they do is completely different.

The trouble with most landscape companies owned by a landscaper is they are dependent on the landscaper. That's because they're sole proprietorships—the smallest, most limited form a company can take. Sole proprietorships are formed around the technician, whether landscaper or roofer.

You may choose in the beginning to form a sole proprietorship, but you should understand its limitations. The company called a *sole proprietorship* depends on the owner—that is, the landscape contractor. The company called a *business* depends on other people plus a system by which that business does what it does. Once your sole proprietorship becomes a business, you can replicate it, turning it into an *enterprise*.

Consider the example of Sea Landscaping. The clients don't come in asking for Douglas Sea, although he is one of the top landscape contractors around. After all, he can only handle so many projects a day and be in only one location at a time.

Yet he wants to offer his high-quality services to more people in the community. If he has reliable systems in place—systems that any qualified subcontractor can learn to use—he has created a business and it can be replicated. Douglas can then go on to offer his services—which demand his guidance, not his presence—in a multitude of different settings. He can open dozens of landscaping companies, none of which need Douglas Sea himself, except in the role of entrepreneur.

Is your landscaping company going to be a sole proprietorship, a business, or an enterprise? Planning is crucial to answering this all-important question. Whatever you choose to do must be communicated by your plan, which is really three interrelated plans in one. We call it the Planning Triangle, and it consists of

- the business plan;
- the job plan; and
- the completion plan.

The three plans form a triangle, with the business plan at the base, the job plan in the center, and the completion plan at the apex.

The business plan determines *who* you are (the business), the job plan determines *what* you do (the specific focus of your landscaping business), and the completion plan determines *how* you do it (the fulfillment process).

By looking at the Planning Triangle, we see that the three critical plans are interconnected. The connection between them is established by asking the following questions:

1. *Who are we?*—purely a strategic question
2. *What do we do?*—both a strategic and a tactical question
3. *How do we do it?*—both a strategic and a tactical question

Strategic questions shape your business's vision and destiny, of which your business is only one essential component. Tactical questions turn that vision into reality. Thus, strategic questions provide the foundation for tactical questions, just as the base provides the foundation for the middle and apex of your Planning Triangle.

First ask: What do we do, and how do we do it *strategically*?

And then: What do we do, and how do we do it *practically*?

Let's look at how the three plans will help you develop your business.

The Business Plan

Your business plan will determine what you choose to do in your landscaping business and the way you choose to do it. Without a business plan, your business can do little more than survive. And even that will take more than a little luck.

Without a business plan, you're treading water in a deep pool with no shore in sight. You're working against the natural flow.

I'm not talking about the traditional business plan taught in business schools. No, this business plan reads like a story—the most important story you will ever tell.

Your business plan must clearly describe

- the business you are creating;
- the purpose it will serve;
- the vision it will pursue;
- the process through which you will turn that vision into a reality; and
- the way money will be used to realize your vision.

Build your business plan with *business* language, not *sole proprietor* language (the landscape contractor's language). Make sure the plan focuses on matters of interest to your lenders and shareholders rather than just your technicians. It should rely on demographics and psychographics to tell you who buys and why; it should also include projections for return on investment and return on equity. Use it to detail both the market and the strategy through which you intend to become a leader in that market, not as a landscape contractor but as a business enterprise.

The business plan, though absolutely essential, is only one of three critical plans every landscape contractor needs to create and implement. Now let's take a look at the job plan.

The Job Plan

The job plan includes everything a landscape contractor needs to know, have, and do to deliver his or her promise to a client on time, every time.

Every task should prompt you to ask three questions:

1. What do I need to know?
2. What do I need to have?
3. What do I need to do?

What Do I Need to Know?

What information do I need to satisfy my promise on time, every time, exactly as promised? To recognize what you need to know, you must understand the expectations and limitations of others, including your clients, administrators, managers, subcontractors, designers, horticulturalists, and other employees. Are you clear on those expectations? Don't make the mistake of assuming you know. Instead, create a need-to-know checklist to make sure you ask all the necessary questions.

A need-to-know checklist might look like this:

- What are my clients' expectations?
- What are my subcontractors' expectations?
- What are my staff's expectations?
- What are my vendors' expectations?

What Do I Need to Have?

This question raises the issue of resources—namely, money, people, and time. If you don't have enough money to finance operations, how can you fulfill those expectations without creating cash-flow problems? If you don't have a sufficient number of people or people with sufficient skills, what happens then? And if you don't have enough time to manage the job to completion, what happens when you can't be in two places at once?

Again, don't assume that you can get what you need when you need it. Most often, you can't. And even if you can get what you need at the last minute, you'll pay dearly for it.

What Do I Need to Do?

The focus here is on actions to be started and finished. *What do I need to do to fulfill the expectations of this client on time, every time, exactly as promised?* For example, what exactly is necessary to build a segmental retaining wall, install a paver patio, or install a landscape plan?

Your clients fall into distinct categories, and those categories make up your business. The best landscaping companies will invariably focus on fewer and fewer categories as they discover the importance of doing one thing better than anyone else. Answering the question *What do I need to do?* demands a series of action plans, including

- the objective to be achieved;
- the standards by which you will know that the objective has been achieved;
- the benchmarks you need to reach for the objective to be achieved;
- the function/person accountable for the completion of the benchmarks;
- the budget for the completion of each benchmark; and
- the time by which each benchmark must be completed.

Your action plans should become the foundation for the completion plans. The reason you need completion plans is to ensure that everything you do is not only realistic but can also be managed.

The Completion Plan

If the job plan gives you results and provides you with standards, the completion plan tells you everything you need to know about every benchmark in the job plan—that is, how you're going to fulfill client expectations on time, every time, as promised. In other words, how you're going to install an irrigation system and educate a client on proper operations.

The completion plan is essentially the operations manual, providing information about the details of doing tactical work. It is a guide to tell the people responsible for doing that work exactly how to do it.

Every completion plan becomes a part of the knowledge base of your business. No completion plan goes to waste. Every completion plan becomes a kind of textbook that explains to new employees or new subcontractors joining your team how your business operates in a way that distinguishes it from all other landscaping companies.

To return to an earlier example, the completion plan for making a Big Mac is explicitly described in the *McDonald's Operation Manual*, as is every completion plan needed to run a McDonald's business.

The completion plan for a landscape contractor might include the step-by-step details of how to lay out a garden based on a scaled drawing or how to organize the supplies for the job to minimize movement of materials or the sequence of steps that create a successful lawn service. Of course, all those who work in landscaping have to watch what their competitors are doing. They've learned to do it the same way everyone else has learned to do it. But if you are going to stand out as unique in the minds of your clients, employees, and others, you must invent your own way of doing even ordinary things. Most of that value-added perception will come from your communication skills, your listening skills, and your innovative skills in transforming an ordinary visit into a great, value-added client experience.

Perhaps you'll decide that a mandatory part of the "as-built" plan will be identifying the color codes for installation and explaining what the different colors and codes mean so clients have a better understanding of the routing of their irrigation plan. If no other landscape contractor your clients have seen has ever taken the time to explain the procedure, you'll immediately set yourself apart. You must constantly raise the questions: *How do we do it here? How should we do it here?*

The quality of your answers will determine how effectively you distinguish your business from every other landscape contractor's business.

Benchmarks

You can measure the movement of your business—from what it is today to what it will be in the future—using business benchmarks.

These are the goals you want your business to achieve during its lifetime.
Your benchmarks should include the following:

- Financial benchmarks
- Emotional benchmarks (the impact your company will have on everyone who comes into contact with it)
- Performance benchmarks
- Client benchmarks (Who are they? Why do they come to you? What will your company give them that no one else will?)
- Employee benchmarks (How do you grow people? How do you find people who want to grow? How do you create a school in your company that will teach your people skills they can't learn anywhere else?)

Your business benchmarks will reflect (1) the position your company will hold in the minds and hearts of your clients, employees, and investors, and (2) how you intend to make that position a reality through the systems you develop.

Your benchmarks will describe how your management team will take shape and what systems you will need to develop so your managers, just like McDonald's managers, will be able to produce the results for which they will be held accountable.

Benefits of the Planning Triangle

By implementing the Planning Triangle, you will discover:

- what your company will look, act, and feel like when it's fully evolved;
- when that's going to happen;
- how much money you will make; and
- much more.

These, then, are the primary purposes of the three critical plans: (1) to clarify precisely what needs to be done to get what the landscape contractor wants from his or her company and life, and (2) to define the specific steps by which it will happen.

First *this* must happen, then *that* must happen. One, two, three. By monitoring your progress, step by step, you can determine whether you're on the right track.

That's what planning is all about. It's about creating a standard—a yardstick—against which you will be able to measure your performance.

Failing to create such a standard is like throwing a straw into a hurricane. Who knows where that straw will land?

Have you taken the leap? Have you accepted that the words *business* and *company* are not synonymous? That a sole proprietorship relies on the landscape contractor and a business relies on other people plus a system?

Because most landscapers are control freaks, 99 percent of today's landscaping companies are sole proprietorships, not businesses.

The result, as a friend of mine says, is that "landscape contractors are spending all day stamping out fires when all around them the forest is ablaze. They're out of touch, and that landscape contractor better take control of the business before someone else does."

Because landscape contractors are never taught to think like entrepreneurs, the landscaping professional is forever at war with the entrepreneur. This is especially evident in large, multi-location companies, where there is no personal relationship with the owner, where bureaucrats (corporate management) often try to control landscape contractors (entrepreneurs). They usually end up treating each other as combatants. In fact, the single greatest reason landscapers become entrepreneurs is to divorce such bureaucrats and to begin to reinvent the landscaping enterprise.

That's you. Now the divorce is over and a new love affair has begun. You're a landscape contractor with a plan! Who wouldn't want to do business with such a person?

Now let's take the next step in our strategic odyssey and take a closer look at the subject of management. But before we do, read what Tony has to say on the subject of planning. ✣

CHAPTER
6

What's Your Plan?

Tony Bass

You can't overestimate the need to plan and prepare. In most of the mistakes I've made, there has been this common theme of inadequate planning beforehand. You really can't over prepare in business!
—Chris Corrigan

W
hy are you working in or thinking about joining the land-scape industry today?

Many of us work in the landscape industry because we have a passionate love of the outdoors. We would rather be outside than inside most of the time. Some of us have a deep connection with seeing and creating beautiful landscapes, and get a real thrill from a weed-free, nicely striped, mowed, edged, and trimmed lawn. Others have affection for agriculture, but live in suburban and urban areas. Landscaping is the nearest thing to farming. And yet a few of us entered this industry because we are attached to the equipment or mechanical side of the business. For others, this is simply the family business.

The above reasons might have gotten you into this industry, but they did not lead you to start a landscape company. Just as Michael E. Gerber so eloquently explained in *The E-Myth*, you entered the world of the landscape company because you had an *entrepreneurial seizure*. You were seeking control, greater opportunity, and the ability to get more from life than you were getting. I will bet that if you clearly understood the financial facts regarding the landscaping industry, you would have chosen another career path.

After all, according to the US Department of Labor Office of Statistics—in the Occupational Employment Statistics 2010—91 percent of jobs in the United States pay higher wages than entry-level landscaping or grounds maintenance jobs, which rank 749th in the survey. In other words, there are a lot higher-paying jobs than in this industry. Unless you join a large firm that has managers within the landscape organization, you could be faced with a life of financial poverty. Sometimes, the truth hurts.

Perhaps you faced the reality of low wages working for a landscape company. You were good at what you were doing. So one day, in a quest for a better life, you had an entrepreneurial seizure and decided that the only way to higher wages was to become the boss.

Answer this question: Why did you get into this business? Write down your answer. This is a small step in building your plan for the future.

My initial goals for starting a landscape company were

- to become a businessman;
- to make a lot of money;
- to avoid working for someone else; and
- to create a truly professional and dedicated landscape design, installation, and maintenance company.

Early in my life, I made an interesting observation. The only people I had ever met who seemed to have a lot of money were business owners. If you have a business, you have to have money, right?

My first five years in business were an incredible education. Mostly, the first five years were a technical education. I was simply learning the trade. I was working in my business. It took me five years of working in the field before I began to look outside of my comfort zone for an answer to the question of growing my business from the inside.

Somewhere between my confusion about money (and accounting) and a serious backache from jumping up and down on shovels, I finally began to look outside for answers. When I think about it, finding *The E-Myth* at that crucial point in time was a miracle. More likely, it was divine intervention.

Have you ever heard this? "When the student is ready, the teacher will appear."

Here is what this quote means to me. Until the student is open and ready to learn, no amount of teachers will be able to teach him anything. Until you are ready to learn, no amount of books, seminars, consultants, advisors, webinars, or mentors will be enough to help you grow personally and professionally. Unfortunately, in many companies, the owner simply has never learned how to plan.

Your ability to learn how to plan is an internal decision. Most landscape companies remain very small because there aren't many owners willing to become lifelong students. If your company is small, it is because your plan is nonexistent, too small, or lacking the key components to help you build a real, successful business.

So what's your plan?

At the time of this writing, approximately ninety-four thousand landscape companies nationwide have about 600,000 employees. Many more companies exist – about 312,000 - where the owner is the only employee. The average landscape company has six to seven employees. Nearly 80 percent of all landscape companies have sales under $1 million per year. Ninety-five percent of all landscape companies have sales under $5 million per year. Your company could make the top 150 list of firms by revenue in the entire United States if sales hit $7 million per year.

Where does your company fit into this industry? Take an inventory of where you are today.

The Bass Team in 1991. An average landscape company working on a new plan.

Soon after I read *The E-Myth*, my mom took a photo of my company. I wanted to document where I was at that point in time. Michael taught me that a great business plan will include three key components:

- Innovation—A plan to create and operate your company in your own unique and special way
- Quantification—A plan to quantify and measure everything you do, then seek improvement
- Orchestration—A plan to precisely detail how to do the work the best possible way

Amazingly, there is a direct correlation between a company's ability to grow, expand, and add revenue and its ability to properly plan for the future. Seldom will you meet an owner of a $5 million-per-year firm without a well-written series of business plans. More often, you will meet an owner of a smaller firm—averaging $575,431 annual revenue and 6.4 employees—who has no written business plan at all.

The US Small Business Administration (SBA) recently conducted a survey on small business. The survey revealed that 80 percent of all business owners reported having no written business plans. I find this statistic suspiciously close to the statistic from the same SBA survey that says 80 percent of small businesses fail within the first five years.

How do you defy the odds and create wealth working in the landscape industry?

Enter the power of planning motivated by your desire to work on your business. Your new goal is to create the perfect franchise prototype within your own firm. This plan will build your business so that it could operate in five hundred different locations. After all, if you own your own business, you can choose how to spend your time, right? This is *The E-Myth* way to business. Let's talk about creating your new future. Let's discuss the planning triangle Michael outlined in chapter 5.

Beginning Your Business Plan

This is the foundation of your business. The first step I use to help a company create a well-written business plan is to challenge the owner with a detailed, confidential questionnaire. This will identify what stage of business development you are currently in and what goals you have for your life. Here is a sample of these questions:

- Do you prepare an annual budget? If no, why not? If yes, what month of the year do you do it?
- How do you arrive at a price for a job? Describe the entire process in detail.
- Do you think this is an accurate procedure? Why or why not?
- What is your current man-hour rate? How did you arrive at this number?
- How often do you check your estimates against your actual job cost? Describe precisely how you do it.
- How much was your total field labor in dollars last year? How many labor hours did you use in the field?
- What was your overhead in dollars last year?
- What is the most common (frequent) work you do in your company? Please include all the owners if you have partnerships in your company.
- Are you satisfied with the amount of money you took home (or your company netted before taxes) last year? If not, what is your personal annual salary goal (or your company net profit goal)?

- Describe your perfect vision for what your company will look like twelve months from now. If you do not know, list ten traits you feel could make your quality of life (or company life) improve dramatically in the next twelve months.
- Describe your perfect vision for what your company will look like three to five years from now.
- What is your favorite thing(s) to do in your company and why?
- What is your least favorite thing(s) to do in your company and why?
- What are your three biggest business problems or challenges?
- Are you having money problems today? Please describe.
- Suppose you have built the perfect business. You have accomplished your goals. At the end of your life, you are attending your own funeral. What do you want your friends, family, and business associates to say about you?

Answering These Questions

Your business plan starts with these thought-provoking questions. These are not simply yes-and-no questions. They are designed to make you think. These questions expose problems within your current processes. Before you go to work again, step away from your company's day-to-day routines. Answer these questions as honestly and as completely as possible. Please note: If you have trouble answering these questions, you are not alone.

Where to Begin

I get calls from contractors all over North America seeking to improve their businesses. They say they want help making their phone ring more frequently. They want help winning contracts without being the lowest bidder. They want help organizing their people to get more done in less time. They want help learning how to work fewer hours and make enough money to support the family.

In every case, I ask them to send me a copy of their business plan, three recent job estimates, and their financial statements.

I am looking for a snapshot of the past, present, and future. My clients always have plenty of recent estimates to send me. Most will have some form of financial statement showing evidence of the past. However, eight times out of ten, there is *no business plan* at all. No plan for the future. Nothing.

However, when I do see a business plan, here is what I usually find: The plan is lacking the key components needed to guide the business. This means that the owner(s) does not have the ability to formulate a business plan. The good news is that this is learnable, teachable, and, most of all, dependable.

Please, take my advice. Do not put yourself, your family, and your business through one more year without a plan for the future. Life is too precious. Time is too short. Work is so hard. Invest in your company by building a rock-solid plan for the future.

My Measurable Business Goals

Earlier in this chapter, I shared my original goals for starting a landscape company. After investing six solid months of building the ultimate detailed business plan for my future landscape company, I had the following list of goals:

- Become the landscape company of choice in middle Georgia for prospective customers and employees
- Continually increase the level of professionalism within my company and the entire landscape industry
- Build a multi-million dollar business that would support a $100,000 annual salary for the president of the firm
- Operate the company with a minimum 10 percent net profit or 25 percent return on assets

- Fulfill our customers' needs by providing timely, quality products and services
- Build a client base that creates 75 percent of income from maintenance revenues and 25 percent of revenue from landscape construction services
- Plan to work five days a week with the exception of the busy spring season and weather-related work interruptions

How do these goals differ from my original goals? The biggest difference is that these goals are measurable. Having financial benchmarks is a key part of building a rock-solid business plan for your future. Remember this: If you can measure it, you can improve it. And so it goes with goals. If your goals are not measurable, you have no way of communicating your achievement of goals.

Build Your Plan in Less than a Week

Your business plan is the best set of written goals for your future that you will ever create. The most amazing thing about having a process for building such a plan is you can do it in less than forty hours. You can invest less than one workweek in changing your future!

The Reason You Have Problems

Poor planning rears its ugly head most often when you are performing daily jobs. You have problems correctly estimating the amount of labor required to complete the project. You have trouble providing your client with a precise schedule of when the job will start and when the job will finish. You have trouble setting daily or hourly goals for your team. You have difficulty allocating the correct amount of equipment to keep the crew operating with maximum productivity.

You constantly struggle to manage the delivery of materials in the right sequence, in the correct quantity, and at the right time from job start to job completion. You lack the capital to purchase all of the supplies needed to finish the job. You are losing valuable hours because you don't have the right tools for the job. If these challenges are inside your company, the problem is really quite simple: You are lacking a well-organized job plan.

The answer to your problems can be found by learning how to use a production rate-based estimating system to accurately plan each job. I'll share more on this in a later chapter.

The Planning Triangle

There are other problems facing you and your firm. These problems show up when you walk through a job site. You want to collect your money but your client says, "This isn't what I expected. I thought you were going to do this. You said you were going to do that. The guys told me one thing on the first day of the job, but it turned out different. This color is wrong. The shape is not what I was expecting. This plant is out of location. The shrubs aren't trimmed like I want. The turf is uneven here. This sprinkler was hitting my window last night and it kept me awake all night. The lighting your guys installed comes on before it gets dark."

Does any of this sound familiar?

You are lacking a well-thought-out job completion plan.

Without the planning triangle, your landscape company can't grow, create wealth, or provide you freedom from daily headaches. You must have a business plan, a job plan, and a completion plan.

Just like building a paver patio or segmental retaining wall with a properly constructed base, your business must have a solid foundation. Without the well-organized job plan, you're running out of pavers before the patio is finished.

My goal is to help you see a bright future. *Your ability to plan is the key to your future.* The success or failure of your plans is realized each time you finish a job and each time you close the books on another tax year. These key events build your professional report card. Your future is in jeopardy without consistently happy clients and consistent profits for your firm.

Now that your plan is coming together, read what Michael has to say about management. ✣

On the Subject of Management

Michael E. Gerber

Good management consists of showing average people how to do the work of superior people.

—John D. Rockefeller

E
very landscape contractor, including Steve, eventually faces the issues of management. Most face it badly.

Why do so many landscape contractors suffer from a kind of paralysis when it comes to dealing with management? Why are so few able to get their landscaping company to work the way they want it to and to run it on time? Why are their managers (if they have any) seemingly so inept?

There are two main problems. First, the landscape contractor usually abdicates accountability for management by hiring an office manager. Thus, the landscape contractor is working hand-in-glove with someone who is supposed to do the managing. But the landscape contractor is unmanageable himself!

The landscape contractor doesn't think like a manager because he doesn't think he is a manager. He's a landscape contractor! He rules the roost. And so he gets the office manager to take care of stuff like scheduling appointments, keeping his calendar, collecting receivables, hiring/firing, and much more.

Second, no matter who does the managing, he or she usually has a completely dysfunctional idea of what it means to manage. They're trying to manage people, contrary to what is needed.

We often hear that a good manager must be a "people person." Someone who loves to nourish, figure out, support, care for, teach, baby, monitor, mentor, direct, track, motivate, and, if all else fails, threaten or beat up his or her people.

Don't believe it. Management has far less to do with people than you've been led to believe.

In fact, despite the claims of every management book written by management gurus (who have seldom managed anything), no one—with the exception of a few bloodthirsty tyrants—has ever learned how to manage people.

And the reason is simple: *People are almost impossible to manage.*

Yes, it's true. People are unmanageable. They're inconsistent, unpredictable, unchangeable, unrepentant, irrepressible, and generally impossible.

Doesn't knowing this make you feel better? Now you understand why you've had all those problems! Do you feel the relief, the heavy stone lifted from your chest?

The time has come to fully understand what management is really all about. Rather than managing *people*, management is really all about managing a *process*, a step-by-step way of doing things, which, combined with other processes, becomes a system. For example:

- The process for on-time scheduling
- The process for answering the telephone
- The process for greeting a client
- The process for organizing client files

Thus, a process is the step-by-step way of doing something over time. Considered as a whole, these processes are a system:

- The on-time scheduling system
- The telephone answering system
- The client greeting system
- The file organization system

Instead of managing people, then, the truly effective manager has been taught a system for managing a process through which people get things done.

More precisely, managers and their people, *together*, manage the processes—the systems—that comprise your business. Management is less about *who* gets things done in your business than about *how* things get done.

In fact, great managers are not fascinated with people but with how things get done through people. Great managers are masters at figuring out how to get things done effectively and efficiently through people using extraordinary systems.

Great managers constantly ask key questions, such as:

- What is the result we intend to produce?
- Are we producing that result every single time?
- If we're not producing that result every single time, why not?
- If we are producing that result every single time, how could we produce even better results?
- Do we lack a system? If so, what would that system look like if we were to create it?
- If we have a system, why aren't we using it?

And so forth.

In short, a great manager can leave the office fully assured that it will run at least as well as it does when he or she is physically in the room.

Great managers are those who use a great management system. It is a system that shouts, "This is *how* we manage here" not "This is *who* manages here."

In a truly effective company, how you manage is always more important than who manages. Provided a system is in place, how you manage is transferable, whereas who manages isn't. *How* you manage can be taught, whereas *who* manages can't be.

When a company is dependent on who manages—Murray, Mary, or Moe—that business is in serious jeopardy. Because when Murray, Mary, or Moe leaves, that business has to start over again. What an enormous waste of time and resources!

Even worse, when a company is dependent on who manages, you can bet all the managers in that business are doing their own thing. What could be more unproductive than ten managers who each manage in a unique way? How in the world could you possibly manage those managers?

The answer is: You can't. Because it takes you right back to trying to manage *people* again.

And, as I hope you now know, that's impossible.

In this chapter, I often refer to managers in the plural. I know that most landscape contractors only have one manager—the office manager. And so you may be thinking that a management system isn't so important in a small landscaping company. After all, the office manager does whatever an office manager does (and thank God, because you don't want to do it).

But if your company is ever going to turn into the business it could become, and if that business is ever going to turn into the enterprise of your dreams, then the questions you ask about how the office manager manages your affairs are critical ones. Because until you come to grips with your dual role as owner and key employee, and the relationship your manager has to those two roles, your company/business/enterprise will never realize its potential. Thus the need for a management system.

Management System

What, then, is a management system?

The E-Myth says that a management system is the method by which every manager innovates, quantifies, orchestrates, and then monitors the systems through which your business produces the results you expect.

According to the E-Myth, a manager's job is simple: *to invent the systems through which the owner's vision is consistently and faithfully manifested at the operating level of the business.*

Which brings us right back to the purpose of your business and the need for an entrepreneurial vision.

Are you beginning to see what I'm trying to share with you? That your business is one single thing? And that all the subjects we're discussing here—money, planning, management, and so on—are all about doing one thing well?

That one thing is the one thing your business is intended to do: distinguish your landscaping company from all others.

It is the manager's role to make certain it all fits. And it's your role as entrepreneur to make sure your manager knows what the business is supposed to look, act, and feel like when it's finally done. As clearly as you know how, you must convey to your manager what you know to be true—your vision, your picture of the business when it's finally done. In this way, your vision is translated into your manager's marching orders every day he or she reports to work.

Unless your manager embraces that vision, you and your people will suffer from the tyranny of routine. And your business will suffer from it too.

Now let's move on to people. Because, as we know, it's people who are causing all our problems. But first let's see how E-Myth management insights affected Tony's landscaping business. ❖

Where's My Manager?

Tony Bass

So much of what we call management consists in making it difficult for people to work.

—Peter F. Drucker

C hances are you need to invest more of your precious time becoming a manager and less of your time acting as a land-scape technician. Here is a good reason why: It pays more to be a good manager than a great technician.

There are countless opportunities to go school to learn the technical aspects of horticulture, turfgrass, irrigation, hardscape construction, and even accounting. But when did your education prepare you to juggle the needs of the customers, employees, vendors, and equipment resources within your firm? Did I hear you right? Did you say, "Never"?

I often get calls from contractors who have reached a stage in their professional development where they are trying to decide whether they should hire a manager. I listen as they say, "I don't have trouble selling. I can sell. I can do the work in the field. In fact, I'm good at it. But I need someone to keep those crews organized. I need someone who can make sure they have all the right materials on the right job site at just the right time. I need someone who can keep the guys working when I'm not there. I need someone who will make sure they do the work right the first time. I need someone with experience. I need me a manager."

Before you make the $30,000 to $80,000 decision (the pay range for managers in the landscape industry today) to hire a manager, you need to answer this question: Do you have everything written down? Yes, I mean everything. Every detail you can imagine.

Of all the things you can do to grow or expand your company, hiring your first manager or your next manager could be the straw that breaks the camel's back. When you make the decision to add this *one* person, your company undergoes an immediate transformation. This transformation empties more landscape contractor bank accounts faster than any equipment purchase.

The instant you add a manager, you take a giant leap into the great unknown. Unless you have a management plan, don't hire a manager. They are expensive and require lots of your time to train, and you probably can't afford one without taking a significant pay cut yourself.

The Management Plan

This tool allows you to hire people with very little experience and get good results. It also allows you to replace people, even key people, in your company as they leave. The management plan is the written policies, plans, and procedures within your company. It is the most liberating tool you will ever create. It is a series of documents to design, describe, and detail the what, why, how, when, and who of doing tasks in your firm.

The management plan starts with writing your company rulebook. Let's title this the Company Policy Manual. In this document, start by answering the questions every single employee has already asked you, and answer questions that future employees will ask you. This manual is another step in building a company that satisfies your vision for the future.

The Company Policy Manual builds consistency and respect within your workforce. It answers questions such as:

- Why does this company exist and when did it start?
- Who are the owners and what are their goals?
- What are the company work hours, workdays, and holidays?
- What are the employee hiring, orientation, training, and termination policies?
- What is expected regarding professional conduct, talking to customers, vendors, and co-workers?
- What are the company benefits?
- How do we deal with equipment, supplies, and company assets?
- How do we answer the phone, record the conversation, and prepare for action?
- How do we know if the company is winning, losing, or just barely surviving?
- What will happen if an employee doesn't follow company policies?

A key piece of this document is the acceptance and acknowledgment of the policy manual terms, which your employees should sign.

I have seen policy manuals from two to well over a hundred pages long in client companies. The longer you operate your company, the more likely it is that your policy manual will grow in length, detail, and value to your firm. Without a written policy manual, your manager(s) will always have questions only you can answer.

Really Getting Organized

Next, you must document the technical work within your company. We start by building an organizational chart, a visual illustration of the work your firm performs. The organizational chart will help you gain clarity within your own mind. This tool also builds clarity within the minds of all who join your firm. The illustration below is an example of how many landscape firms are organized. Notice that we organize work by function and not by people. Job functions do not change, but people do. So think about how you can organize your work by function.

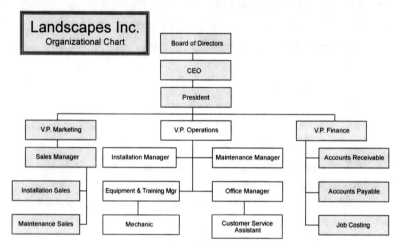

You may look at this and say, "I don't have twenty employees. I don't have a management team. I do all the work myself. Why in the world would I need an organization chart?"

It's simple, really. If you organize your thoughts you can organize your company's work. This chart gives you a roadmap for organized growth. As you increase the volume of work in your firm, part-time functions become full-time functions.

As you (or others) do the part-time functions, you document what you do, why you do it, how you do it, when you do it, and who's involved. The more details you put in writing, the easier it becomes for you to hire for a position or replace an employee if the time comes.

The chart above could represent your firm's management system. However, you might need more specific organization within, say, your firm's field operations. Let's look at how you can best organize one department of your landscaping business.

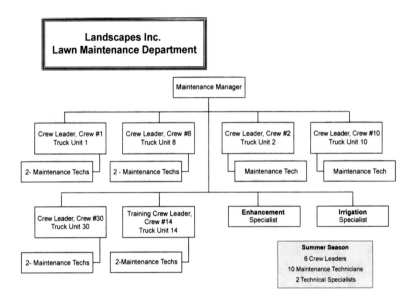

At this point you are getting ready for a manager. You are really building clarity at the operational level of your company.

Now you need job descriptions for each position within the firm. Start at the bottom of your firm with the people responsible for doing the work for which your customers are willing to pay. The plan starts by defining the roles and responsibilities of the landscape maintenance, installation, irrigation, enhancement, and hardscape technicians.

If your firm only provides landscape installation services, that's fine—start with the landscape installation technician. If your firm only provides lawn maintenance services, that's fine too—start with the lawn maintenance technician. Until you clearly document exactly what it means to do these technical jobs with great precision, excellent quality, and professional safety standards, your new manager is going to struggle.

Why will your manager struggle? The struggle comes from an employee being caught somewhere between being a manager, a crew leader, and a technician. The manager really can't be a manager if he doesn't know what to manage. The reason you are likely having trouble growing your business is not because you lack a manager, but you lack the systems that a great manager will need.

Did you hear those new words? I mentioned *crew leaders* (some firms prefer *foremen*). That's a completely different position than manager for your firm. And these positions must be clearly defined, just like all the technicians listed above. You must define the position for your crew leaders so they understand what they do, how they do it, when they do it, why they do it, and how they know the job was completed correctly.

The manager, most likely you, is the only person who can answer all these questions in your business's early stages. The answers are inside your head. But the questions keep coming from outside—technicians, crew leaders, customers, and vendors. Until you capture the answers on paper or in a digital format, you will always have to answer them yourself.

If you hire a manager and you don't give him or her your answers, your company is going to change. Your company is going to start acting like your manager, and a lot less like you. Now this could be good, but most likely, this is bad, if you started this company and the new manager changes it. When he or she makes decisions inconsistent with what you promise employees, vendors, and customers, you're left with the mess.

And guess what? There is nothing worse for a business than to be inconsistent in serving customers, employees, and vendors. When you hire any manager, you must have a detailed business plan that explains what must be managed, how it should be managed, and how to measure success within the crew, department, branch, and company.

Without a detailed management plan, you are better served to hire a personal assistant to handle repetitive tasks, document your daily activities, and help you build the foundation required for a professional manager. Written policies, plans, and procedures provide the company with the one thing you seek from a manager: consistency in and from your company.

Working On The Business

Your management plan will require you to spend more time than you could ever imagine working on your business. Why did I tell you that I took a six-month sabbatical after reading *The E-Myth?* It wasn't because I took one week for writing a business plan and then twenty-five weeks for lying on the beach. It was because the majority of the six months was spent documenting the policies and procedures within every conceivable job and future position in my firm.

It took six months because when it was completed, the documentation contained nearly four hundred pages of information that had been trapped inside my brain. Your management plan will allow you the freedom to answer questions correctly—once—and then preserve those answers for all who come into your company in the future.

I will never forget the harsh reality that Michael shared with me regarding management. The words slapped me across my face. "You can't manage people," he said. "You must manage a process." He was correct again.

Consistency Is the Key to Success

I'll say it again. *Inconsistency within your company will cost you customers every single time.* It is a worthwhile goal for your growing business to simply be consistent in service. You can become successful by being consistent. And you can gauge your success with consistency in two ways: Your ability to satisfy and keep customers, and your ability to retain a dependable workforce.

Consistency is even more important than being great. If inconsistency doesn't cost you customers, it will certainly cost you employees.

Your firm's future is determined by your ability to manage your customers, employees, equipment, and vendors. Your management plan must document the steps to manage each of these four resource categories.

I recently worked with a mentor who has managed several companies with sales more than $100 million per year. I asked him what separates $1 million companies from $100 million companies. He said, "Tony, it's the quality of the policies, plans, and procedures. Big companies get bigger because they continually improve documentation. Small companies stay small because they lack written policies, plans, and procedures. It's that simple."

Manage Processes, Not People

Remember that detailed questionnaire I mentioned I require of new clients? One item on that questionnaire helps me identify the company that lacks a management plan: "Do you have key people or key positions in your company? Explain each."

Nine times out of ten, my clients list the names of the top two or three people in their firm. Then they describe what the person does. But one out of ten sees the important difference. You must have key *positions* first. If you are always focused on key *people*, you will often get your feelings hurt. People leave; positions don't.

Does this help build a new level of clarity inside your mind? It should.

So before you step out on a limb by hiring a manager, invest in building your policies, plans, and procedures. This decision provides you with the strong foundation your firm needs and enables you to manage the work and your employees. You will need those employees if your business is to grow. And grow it will.

Let's take a look as Michael teaches us about people in the next chapter. ✤

9

On the Subject of People

Michael E. Gerber

Very few people go to the doctor when they have a cold. They go to the theatre instead.

—Oscar Wilde

Every landscape contractor I've ever met has complained about people.

About employees: "They come in late, they use the company trucks to go visit their girlfriends, they smoke dope at lunch time and steal gasoline, and they go home early. They have the focus of an antique camera!"

About subcontractors: "Who knows what they do with their time—but they certainly know how to charge for it!"

About suppliers: "They can never make deliveries on time!"

About their clients: "They want me to repair years of bad habits and inadequate turf care!" or "Even if they had a mind, they wouldn't be able to make it up!"

People, people, people. Every landscape contractor's nemesis. And at the heart of it all are the people who work for you.

"By the time I tell them how to do it, I could have done it twenty times myself!" "How come nobody listens to what I say?" "Why is it nobody ever does what I ask them to do?"

Does this sound like you?

So what's the problem with people? To answer that, think back to the last time you walked into a landscape contractor's office. What did you see in the people's faces?

Most people working in landscaping are harried. You can see it in their expressions. They're negative. They're tired. They're humorless. And with good reason! After all, they're surrounded by people all day long who have money problems, marital issues, or trouble with their children. Clients are looking for nurturing, for empathy, for care. And *many* landscape contractors are frustrated with not getting the same level of respect from their clients.

Is it any wonder employees at most landscaping companies are disgruntled? They're surrounded by unhappy people all day. They're answering the same questions 24/7. And most of the time, the owner or the manager has no time for them. He or she is too busy leading a dysfunctional life.

Working with people brings great joy—and monumental frustration. And so it is with landscape contractors and their people. But why? And what can we do about it?

Let's look at the typical landscape contractor—who this person is and isn't.

Most landscape contractors are unprepared to use other people to get results. Not because they can't find people, but because they are fixated on getting the results themselves. In other words, most landscape contractors are not the businesspeople they need to be, but *technicians suffering from an entrepreneurial seizure.*

Am I talking about you? What were you doing before you became an entrepreneur?

Were you a landscape subcontractor working at a large, multi-office organization? A midsized company? A small business?

Didn't you imagine owning your own company as the way out?

Didn't you think that because you knew how to do the technical work—because you knew so much about landscape design, soil, and irrigation—that you were automatically prepared to create a company that does that type of work?

Didn't you figure that by creating your own sole proprietorship you could dump the boss once and for all? How else to get rid of that impossible person, the one driving you crazy, the one who never let you do your own thing, the one who was the main reason you decided to take the leap into a business of your own in the first place?

Didn't you start your own company so you could become your own boss?

And didn't you imagine that once you became your own boss, you would be free to do whatever you wanted to do—and to take home *all* the money?

Honestly, isn't that what you imagined? So you went into business for yourself and immediately dived into work.

Doing it, doing it, doing it.

Busy, busy, busy.

Until one day you realized (or maybe not) that you were doing all of the work. You were doing everything you knew how to do, plus a lot more you knew nothing about. Building sweat equity, you thought.

In reality, you were a technician suffering from an entrepreneurial seizure.

You were just hoping to make a buck in your own company. And sometimes you did earn a wage. But other times you didn't. You were the one signing the checks, all right, but they went to other people.

Does this sound familiar? Is it driving you crazy?

Well, relax, because we're going to show you the right way to do it this time.

Read carefully. Be mindful of the moment. You are about to learn the secret you've been waiting for all your working life.

The People Law

It's critical to know this about the working life of landscape contractors who own their own landscaping company: *Without people, you don't own a company, you own a job.* And it can be the worst job in the world because you're working for a lunatic! (Nothing personal—but we've got to face facts.)

Let me say what every landscape contractor knows: Without people, you're going to have to do it all yourself. Without human help, you're doomed to try to do too much. This isn't a breakthrough idea, but it's amazing how many landscape contractors ignore the truth. They end up knocking themselves out, ten to twelve hours a day. They try to do more, but less actually gets done.

The load can double you over and leave you panting. In addition to the work you're used to doing, you may also have to do the books. And the organizing. And the filing. You'll have to do the planning and the scheduling. When you own your own company, the daily minutiae are never ceasing—as I'm sure you've found out. Like painting the Golden Gate Bridge, it's endless. Which puts it beyond the realm of human possibility. Until you discover how to get it done by somebody else, it will continue on and on until you're a burned-out husk.

But with others helping you, things will start to drastically improve. If, that is, you truly understand how to engage people in the work you need them to do. When you learn how to do that, when you learn how to replace yourself with other people—people trained in your system—then your company can really begin to grow. Only then will you begin to experience true freedom yourself.

What typically happens is that landscape contractors, knowing they need help answering the phone, filing, and so on, go out and find people who can do these things. Once they delegate these duties, however, they rarely spend any time with the hoi polloi. Deep down, they feel it's not important how these things get done; it's only important that they get done.

They fail to grasp the requirement for a system that makes people their greatest asset rather than their greatest liability. A system so reliable that if Chris dropped dead tomorrow, Leslie could do exactly what Chris did. That's where the People Law comes in.

The People Law says that each time you add a new person to your company using an intelligent (turnkey) system that works, you expand your reach. And you can expand your reach almost infinitely! People allow you to be everywhere you want to be simultaneously, without actually having to be there in the flesh.

People are to a landscape contractor what a record was to Frank Sinatra. A Sinatra record could be (and still is) played in a million places at the same time, regardless of where he was. And every record sale produced royalties for Sinatra (or his estate).

With the help of other people, Sinatra created a quality recording that faithfully replicated his unique talents, then made sure it was marketed and distributed, and the revenue managed.

Your people can do the same thing for you. All you need to do is to create a "recording"—a system—of your unique talents, your special way of practicing landscaping, and then replicate it, market it, distribute it, and manage the revenue.

Isn't that what successful businesspeople do? Make a "recording" of their most effective ways of doing business? In this way, they provide a turnkey solution to their clients' problems. A system solution that really works.

Doesn't your company offer the same potential for you that records did for Sinatra (and now for his heirs): The ability to produce income without having to go to work every day?

Isn't that what your people could be for you? The means by which your system for practicing landscaping could be faithfully replicated?

But first you've got to have a system. You have to create a unique way of doing business that you can teach to your people, that you can manage faithfully, and that you can replicate consistently, just like McDonald's.

Because without such a system, without such a "recording," without a unique way of doing business that really works, all you're left with is people doing their own thing. And that is almost always a recipe for chaos. Rather than guaranteeing consistency, it encourages mistake after mistake after mistake.

And isn't that how the problem started in the first place? People doing whatever *they* perceived they needed to do, regardless of what you wanted? People left to their own devices with no regard for the costs of their behavior? The costs to you?

In other words, people without a system.

Can you imagine what would have happened to Frank Sinatra if he had followed that example? If every one of his recordings had been done differently? Imagine a million different versions of "My Way." It's unthinkable.

Would you buy a record like that? What if Frank was having a bad day? What if he had a sore throat?

Please hear this: The People Law is unforgiving. Without a systematic way of doing business, people are more often a liability than an asset. Unless you prepare, you'll find out too late which ones are which.

The People Law says that without a specific system for doing business; without a specific system for recruiting, hiring, and training your people to use that system; and without a specific system for managing and improving your systems, your company will always be a crapshoot.

Do you want to roll the dice with your company at stake? Unfortunately, that is what most landscape contractors are doing.

The People Law also says that you can't effectively delegate your responsibilities unless you have something specific to delegate. And that something specific is a way of doing business that works!

Frank Sinatra is gone, but his voice lives on. And someone is still counting his royalties. That's because Sinatra had a system that worked.

Do you? Now move on to the subject of landscape subcontractors. But first let's see what Tony has to say about people. ✤

CHAPTER 10

Are You Looking for Better People?

Tony Bass

Great minds discuss ideas; average minds discuss events; small minds discuss people.

— Eleanor Roosevelt

There are two things every business owner is always looking for: better customers and better employees. The challenge to find better customers is solved with better and more effective marketing. And guess what? The challenge to find better employees also is solved with better and more effective marketing. *You must be prepared to sell the idea that your company is a great place to work.*

You tend to get better customers if you get more customers. When you add customers, you begin to notice the subtle differences between them. One customer always pays on time. Another always pays late. One customer always asks for discounts. Another never questions the invoice. Over time, you tend to treat the better customers, well, better.

The same thing applies to employees.

You tend to get better employees if you hire more employees. The fact is, until you have a few dozen customers, you won't know a good one from a great one. Until you have a dozen, two dozen, three dozen, or more employees, you really can't be sure you have average, good, or great employees.

Here is a thought-provoking question: Do you have better employees than the staff working at the local fast-food restaurant? You know the ones I am talking about? These are high school part-timers, the high school dropouts, and the first-time employees who are working for minimum wage. Do you believe your employees are more capable than the local fast-food team? They better be.

Landscape contracting is one of the most physically demanding professions in our society. You know this if you have done landscaping work for a few weeks or a few months. It does not take years of experience to know how physically demanding the field can be.

I've had the opportunity to hire a few hundred employees in my career as a landscape contractor. Most of these employees filled the role of a lawn maintenance technician or a landscape installation technician (more on job descriptions in a moment). I will never forget the young man who answered my help-wanted ad just before one spring season. He had made it through the application process, the pre-employment screening process, the verification of past employment process, the group presentation, the driver's history, and a drug-screening check.

Not only was he qualified for the entry-level position advertised, he was qualified to become a crew leader (or foreman) within a few months of in-house and on-the-job training. And he was scheduled for a final interview with me, the firm's president.

He walked in, shook my hand firmly, and said, "Pleased to meet you, Mr. Bass." My eyes must have given away my concerns about his physical appearance right away. The young man must have weighed between 260 and 270 pounds, and he was no more than five feet, eight inches tall—my height.

I asked him why he had applied for a job that would be extremely difficult for a person in his physical condition. He said, "I want this job because I want to lose weight. I need something physical to do. I want to walk behind a lawn mower. I need to get paid while I exercise."

I said, "I have never seen guys your size make it through a summer doing this type of work. It just gets too hot, too physically demanding, and too tiring on our ten-hour workdays."

He said, "The wife and I just had our second child. If I don't get this weight off, I will have a hard time supporting my family for the rest of my life. Please give me a chance. I have put a lot of work into trying to get this job."

I asked him questions about the topics covered in our pre-employment group meeting and a few questions about his past employment, but most of our fifteen or twenty minutes were spent talking about his personal goal of losing weight and how the opportunity to work at my landscaping company could help with that.

I was still skeptical, but I hired him anyway. There was no reason to disqualify him other than his weighing eighty to ninety pounds more than our average field worker. He was assigned to one of my branch offices and introduced to his branch manager. I will never forget the sly grin on the face of that branch manager when he was introduced to "Big Boy."

About two months later, I had a team meeting scheduled at the branch. Before the meeting started, I was discussing a few issues about the meeting with the branch manager when the team of thirty-five employees filed into the shop. I turned to the branch manager and said, "I don't recognize the guy in the second row. When did you hire him?"

The branch manager said, "Big Boy has dropped forty-five pounds! You hired him, remember?"

"Wow, he stuck with you after all! I can't believe how skinny his face looks. Forty-five pounds in two months? Amazing!" I said.

This is an example of how physically demanding the work of a landscape contractor really is. But two important lessons about hiring people can be learned from this story: (1) We used an employee screening and evaluation system to identify the best employment prospects, and (2) we provided a person a job that matched well with his personal goals.

To get good employees, you must have a documented process to recruit, evaluate, hire, train, and retain team members with the least amount of effort. To get great employees, you must create a win-win situation for good people to want to join your firm. To get great employees, working at your firm has to be "much more than a job."

Better Than Average

Think of employees like this. You can't be certain how good any particular employee is until you have someone else doing the same job and producing better results. There is a difference from person to person, and the more people you hire, the easier it becomes to see the difference.

How do you get people to do what *you* want them to do? This is one of the great challenges of business. It always has been and it always will be.

Here is your answer: You can't get people to do anything *you* want them do. When Michael explained this concept in *The E-Myth*, I immediately began to feel better about myself.

When I started my company and became a business owner, I had no idea about the challenges I would face in recruiting, hiring, and retaining employees. My mind was clouded with my personal experiences.

As a young man, I watched my father and his approach to work. I saw a man get up, put on his tie, and report to his first assignment promptly before 8 a.m. every single day (excluding holidays and vacations) of every single week of every year. I *assumed* that every red-blooded American with a job acted the same way. I *assumed* that when a person was given a job, he or she simply performed that job with great enthusiasm, dependability, and consistency. After all, that's what Dad did for the Xerox Corporation for thirty-five years.

As a young student, I worked at my grandpa's construction company each summer. Before I could drive, Mom or Dad would drop me off every day at the job site, right on time, until school started back up. I can't say that I was always enthusiastic about picking up trash, carrying heavy loads of lumber, or retrieving tools from the trucks, but I sure was consistent and dependable.

Later, as a high school and college student, I found a great-paying part-time job that allowed me to work around my school schedule. The grocery store managers were experts at coordinating school schedules for part-time workers with the grocery store's work needs. And guess how I behaved at that job? I showed up for work every day I was scheduled, and I showed up on time for the next seven years. I stuck with that job until I received my bachelor's degree. That's the way it is supposed to work in business, right? You get a job, you show up on time, and you keep it. Well, that's what I thought.

When I started the landscape company, I faced a real challenge. I needed to hire some help. The first source I tapped was my old high school and college friends. After all, a couple of them needed a job, and I needed some help. The problem came later, when I faced the reality that they did not look at my landscape company as a career opportunity but as a temporary fix for their cash needs until school started again or until they found a better-paying job. And they left. So I needed to hire some help, again.

And so it goes with the small business owner. People come and people go. Each time the people come, it creates work. There are forms to fill out. There are uniforms to issue. And you have to train these new people.

Each time people go, it creates work. You must recruit, find, hire, and then train new people all over again. How on earth do you figure the cost of doing this kind of work in your pricing system, on your bids, or within your quotes? How do you find time to perform the jobs your customers are willing to pay for when you have to deal with these employee issues? Stick with me. Your answers are coming.

I remember being interviewed by a business consultant after I had been operating my company for about four years. He asked me the question he was asking a number of small business owners in preparation to write his book: "What has been the biggest surprise or the greatest learning experience as a small business owner?" My answer:

"I have learned that just because you hire someone, it doesn't mean they will work. It doesn't mean they will stay with you. It doesn't mean they will do their best."

Although the statements I made above are true, I did not know what I did not know.

After reading *The E-Myth*, I was equipped with a new people strategy. I began to understand what I did not know about people and the systems needed to fix my people problems. I needed to create a business that was better than average. In a business that was better than average, I could create a desire for better-than-average people to come to work, to try hard, and to stay longer than the employees I hired in my early years as an employer.

Finding Your Team of Superstars

For you to build a world-class team that will allow your business to work because of you, you need a turnkey people process. Without a well-organized people process, your business will only work when you work. You don't just need more or better people, you need a system.

Here is an overview of my people system that can build a world-class team of superstar employees. This includes the processes of

- recruiting;
- application;
- screening;
- selling the company as a "great place to work";
- interviewing;
- job descriptions and the job offer;
- orientation;
- training;
- evaluation; and
- repeat, repeat, repeat.

The Recruiting Process

Recruiting employees is an ongoing responsibility for growing companies and for companies who seek continuous improvement. You should recruit prospects every year. Due to the seasonal nature of this business, the winter season or pre-spring season is the perfect time to recruit. By letting your existing group of employees know you are always looking for better people, you create awareness that it's not "their job." When you commit to recruiting each year, you use the strategy world-class sports teams use to bring home national championships.

Recruiting employees is really a marketing function. You use a variety of strategies to build awareness that your firm has job opportunities. Recruiting should include help-wanted advertising, online social media announcements, company job opportunity handouts placed in (or on) all trucks, posting with your state's department of labor, posting within your firm, posting with online employment sites, posting on your company website, posting within your professional green industry associations, announcements to your clients and vendors, and posting and participating in job fairs with schools, colleges, and universities. To get top candidates, you need a lot of prospects with a variety of backgrounds. Your ability to find superstar employees is directly tied to the number of prospects you can persuade to apply for employment.

The application process is designed to help you organize prospective employee information. Yes, you must always get the basics of contact information and educational and work history. But that's not enough. For you to identify superstars, you need to put the standard application on steroids. You need to challenge the candidate with practical tests. The application tests should include horticultural questions, tool identification, math problems, situational responses, and writing answers to open-ended questions. These tests, which should focus on the technical portion of your company's work, begin the screening process.

The Screening Process

This part is critical; you want the top applicants for all positions, both entry-level and managers. When hiring technicians, managers, leaders, and salespeople, the stakes are high and bad hires can cost you thousands of dollars. Include professionally developed pre-employment screening tests or personality profile exams in the initial application for employment. The pre-employment screening tests give the business owner, recruiter, or manager an objective way to compare one prospect with another. Using the tools of a human resources professional, the owner or manager can avoid wasting time interviewing applicants who are not qualified or do not possess the skills needed for the organization. This way, you don't have to rely solely on your "gut feeling" from an interview to make a hiring decision.

If you have dozens or hundreds of applicants, a well-organized application and screening process will be able to identify top prospects quickly. But can you hire the top prospects? Or do your competitors always seem to get the best employees? Selling the company process is how good companies get great employees.

Recruitment Events

Here's how you improve your personal productivity and avoid spending hours in interviews. Create an event where you will present your company to a group of prospective employees. You might call this a "job fair." Stand before the group and introduce yourself. Tell your company story and your vision for your company's future, and why great people want to work at your firm. Provide an overview of the various jobs within your firm.

Invite ten times the number of prospects you actually intend to hire. You want to create the awareness that lots of people are interested in working at your firm. Plan the event well in advance and make use of every recruiting strategy identified above.

Your job is to sell your company as a great place to work, with great opportunities for employees, and then to do your best to scare the weak applicants away. I suggest you create a slideshow that includes photos of people working for your firm, before and after photos from job sites, equipment in operation, illustrations regarding your company structure, and your company history. Describe the various jobs within the company and the pay ranges for each, and then ask the applicants to write down which job they feel they are best qualified to apply for that day. This way, you give the prospects a chance to self-evaluate and choose which jobs(s) they are best qualified. People like to be in control.

Begin by painting a rosy picture. You want to put your company in the best possible light as a reputable firm with opportunities for advancement as you build the team. Then transition to the realities of working in a landscape company—working outdoors and the risks involved with such a job. Be up front and let the entire group know that this is a seasonal business and only the best of the best are offered full-time, year-round employment. Always use true stories to illustrate a point.

I will never forget the reaction I got to my snake photo and story at recruitment meetings. It goes like this:

"By now you can see that our company is a great place to work and offers significant opportunities to make money. However, there are risks working outdoors. For example, you can easily get sunburned, or be exposed to poison ivy, fire ants, mosquitoes, and even spiders. If you are even a bit squeamish with the thought of working with fertilizer and pesticides, you should withdraw your application.

"Take a look at this photo. One of our irrigation technicians recently went out on a service call where the irrigation pump had quit working. He went out into the lake to remove it and as he pulled it up out of the water, a huge water moccasin appeared, stuck inside and attached to the pump! The good news is his head was chopped off and ground up inside the pump intake. Although it's rare, working outside has its dangers, including snakes.

"So if any of this makes you uncomfortable, I ask that you simply leave now and tell the team member at the back of the room to withdraw your application. For everyone else, we will be posting interview schedules for today at the back room within the next fifteen minutes. We invite you to enjoy refreshments until we get the interview schedule posted. Please stick around and see if you will be offered an interview, what time to be here today, and what you can do to improve your chances to be hired for immediate openings. Thank you for coming out today and applying to work here. Good luck to each of you!"

Invariably, I would have one, two, or three people get up and walk out after seeing the snake photo and hearing the story. It weeded out the weak applicants and added an element of surprise to the entire employment screening process.

You might be shaking your head and saying, "I can't get ten applicants to show up at the same time" or "I don't have a nice facility to bring ten people together for a meeting and slideshow." Others say, "I don't have time to plan such an event" or "I only need one person right now. I don't need five, ten, or twenty employees."

Here's my response. I have used this exact process when the unemployment rate in the United States was less than 5 percent and most small business owners said there were no employees to be found. I have used this process to recruit and screen fifty applicants in one eight-hour shift and still have time to be at home to watch the six o'clock news. I have used this process to ramp up from forty to eighty employees just in time for the spring season over a two-week period. Can you add forty employees in two weeks and not have your entire company blow up? You can now.

The Interview Process

The interview process can be completed in fifteen to twenty minutes. No more hour-long interviews with one prospective employee. The plan is to only interview prospects who have met the basic qualifications. Ask each applicant the same basic questions:

- Tell me about a time when you loved your job and your work.
- Why did you leave your last job(s)?
- Why do you want to work here?

With a written set of questions, anyone can complete the interview. By using the same questions for all interviews, you and the other interviewers can compare answers from one applicant to another. With a process, you can get consistent results. You can select people like Big Boy. You will find qualified people with goals that match your company's needs. And now, you must complete the sales process.

Job Descriptions and the Job Offer Process

Job descriptions and the offer process close the deal with top prospects. You set expectations about what the employees will be doing, how they will do it successfully, and what they must accomplish to move up in the company. In the landscape industry, we must recruit young, physically fit applicants to handle the field jobs. The way you stand out to the best candidates is to provide a written job offer. Yes, put all job offers in writing.

The job offer should include the following: job title, start date, pay rate, benefits package, to whom the recruits will report, what training will be provided, when they will be evaluated, and how they can move up to the next position within your firm. Part of building a world-class company is to retain talent. To retain talent, you must create an awareness of how employees move up in the firm on day one with the written offer.

The Orientation Process

The orientation process sets the expectations for the employees' entire employment lifespan. What does the first day of employment look like for your employees? You only have one chance to make a first impression. You must make it the same way with each person who buys into joining your firm. The first day of employment should entail a checklist of activities that includes a proper introduction to your firm and your initial training process. This process should include filling out employment forms, taking a facility tour, reading your company policy manual, reading the job description, watching training videos, taking written tests verifying an understanding of the materials, reading your company technical training manuals, assigning uniforms, and introducing equipment, customer service policies, and physical operation of tools by an experienced employee.

If day one, hour one at your company begins with, "Get in the truck. José will show you what to do when you get there," your orientation and initial training process will be inadequate. You will face high turnover of employees. As time passes, you will feel like there is something wrong with you.

The Evaluation Process

Your evaluation helps you retain the best of the best. Athletes get immediate evaluation. Their evaluators keep score and time so they understand very quickly how they compare with the competition. Your job as a business owner will include providing feedback to employees. But understand that you, the owner, are not the only person who provides the feedback. Feedback comes from an immediate supervisor, first and foremost. The immediate supervisor will make a decision to keep or release the new employee within the first thirty days of employment.

However, evaluation continues from clients, vendors, and fellow crewmembers. It occurs each month from client satisfaction surveys. Evaluation occurs as equipment is used and safety policies are followed. It occurs as the firm's financial performance is reported in company meetings. Evaluation never stops! Everyone must always contribute to continuous improvement.

Repeat, Repeat, Repeat

The people process never ends. As people come and go, the process repeats. To retain a team of superstar employees, you must repeat, repeat, and repeat.

Communicate and educate with company meetings. Your entire staff must know your progress as a company. Let's call this "keeping score" in your game of business. Communicate with your managers on the progress of your existing people. When people stop growing, your company stops growing. So you must help them grow. Repeat constantly the internal training systems that teach the basics of equipment safety, horticulture, customer service, sales, estimating, and much more.

When you identify people who don't buy into the system, cut them loose. Let them go. Fire the weak players. Build yourself a better team. Your future, your freedom, and your life depend on it.

Your company can become a world-class organization by committing to training. Your organization can become world-class by offering the basic services of landscaping, lawn maintenance, irrigation, hardscaping, or tree service by executing without mistakes. Simply make a commitment to ongoing training for your team. Then your people will get better because of you. The people process should include weekly, monthly, seasonal, and annual training initiatives.

Combine Training and Evaluation

Here is an example of how to combine the evaluation process with your repetitive training process. Offer special training opportunities and see who chooses to participate.

For example, post a "notice of scholarship" to receive paid training to attend a state, regional, or national landscape industry education event. Have an application form and a limited number of winners, and make a big deal of the opportunity. Then see who applies.

When you encourage your team members to seek personal improvement and take their career to the next level, you are building loyalty, respect, trust, and commitment. The secret to superstars is to grow them internally. Very few of them knock on your door, but with the system, you are in control. You shape your own destiny.

Are you starting to see what it takes to build a world-class landscaping firm? Do you understand that building a company that works begins with building a process that works? Can you comprehend that you must have your company vision clear in your own mind before it can be clear in your employees' minds? Clarity provides consistency. Consistency provides control.

The People Strategy

The People Strategy can be summarized as follows. You must define a complete process for people to understand why you exist, your purpose, what they do, how they do it, when they do it, why they do it, and how will they know they have done it correctly. And you must always seek improvement within the organization over time.

Getting your people to do what you want them do is not easy. This is serious work that could take weeks, months, or years to fully develop on your own. However, the key to building a world-class firm is determined by your vision and your ability to share that vision with your people.

Your people become your ticket to a more predictable company. Your people give you leverage. Your people give you more time to spend with your family, your passions, and your dreams. You simply can't do it all by yourself, and I don't want you to have to do it all by yourself.

To get help implementing your People Strategy, visit www.michaelegerber.com/co-author. Now let's see what Michael has to say about subcontractors. ✤

CHAPTER

11

On the Subject of Subcontractors

Michael E. Gerber

*Associate yourself with men of good quality if you esteem your own
reputation, for 'tis better to be alone than in bad company.*
—George Washington

If you're a sole practitioner—that is, you're selling only yourself—then your landscaping company called a *sole proprietorship*
will never make the leap to a landscaping company called a *business.*
The progression from sole proprietorship to business to enterprise
demands that you hire other landscape contractors to do what you
do (or don't do). Contractors call these people subcontractors.

Contractors know that subs can be a huge problem. It's no less
true for landscapers. Until you face this special business problem,
your company will never become a business, and your business will
certainly never become an enterprise.

Long ago, God said, "Let there be landscape contractors.
And so they never forget who they are in my creation, let them

be damned forever to hire people exactly like themselves." Enter the subcontractors.

Solving the Subcontractor Problem

Let's say you're about to hire a landscape subcontractor. Someone who has specific skills: plant identification, sod laying, tree pruning, irrigation, pesticide calibration, whatever. It all starts with choosing the right personnel. After all, these are people to whom you are delegating your responsibility and for whose behavior you are completely liable. Do you really want to leave that choice to chance? Are you that much of a gambler? I doubt it.

If you've never worked with your new subcontractor, how do you really know he or she is skilled? For that matter, what does "skilled" mean?

For you to make an intelligent decision about this subcontractor, you must have a working definition of the word *skilled*. Your challenge is to know *exactly* what your expectations are, then to make sure your other landscape contractors operate with precisely the same expectations. Failure here almost assures a breakdown in your relationship.

I want you to write the following on a piece of paper: "By *skilled*, I mean . . . ." Once you create your personal definition, it will become a standard for you, your company, your clients, and your landscape subcontractors.

A standard, according to Merriam-Webster's Collegiate Dictionary, *Eleventh Edition*, is something "set up and established by authority as a rule for the measure of quantity, weight, extent, value, or quality."

Thus, your goal is to establish a measure of quality control, a standard of skill, which you will apply to all your landscape subcontractors. More important, you are also setting a standard for your company's performance.

By creating standards for your selection of other landscape contractors—standards of skill, performance, integrity, financial stability, and experience—you have begun the powerful process of building a business that can operate exactly as you expect it to.

By carefully thinking about exactly what to expect, you have already begun to improve your business.

In this enlightened state, you will see the selection of your subcontractors as an opportunity to define what you (1) intend to provide for your clients, (2) expect from your employees, and (3) demand for your life.

Powerful stuff, isn't it? Are you up to it? Are you ready to feel your rising power?

Don't rest on your laurels just yet. Defining those standards is only the first step you need to take. The second step is to create a *landscape subcontractor development system.*

A subcontractor development system is an action plan designed to tell you what you are looking for in a landscape subcontractor. It includes the exact benchmarks, accountabilities, timing of fulfillment, and budget you will assign to the process of looking for subcontractors, identifying them, recruiting them, inter-viewing them, training them, managing their work, auditing their performance, compensating them, reviewing them regularly, and terminating or rewarding them for their performance.

All of these things must be documented—actually *written down*—if they're going to make any difference to you, your land-scape subcontractors, your managers, or your bank account!

And then you've got to persist with that system, come hell or high water. Just as Ray Kroc did. Just as Walt Disney did. Just as Sam Walton did.

This leads us to our next topic of discussion: the subject of *estimating*. But first, read what Tony has to say on the subject of landscape subcontractors. ✤

CHAPTER 12

Should You Hire Subcontractors?

Tony Bass

I've been blessed to find people who are smarter than I am, and they help me to execute the vision I have.

—Russell Simmons

You might be saying, "I *am* a subcontractor. I work for builders, general contractors, and property management firms. I don't need to hire subs. I am the guy who actually does the work. I am not the guy who hires someone else to do the work."

The longer you stay in the business of landscape contracting, the more likely you will develop subcontractor relationships. Why? Here are the most common reasons:

- Your client asks you to provide a service you are not licensed to do.

- Your client asks you to provide a service you are not insured to do.

103

- Your client asks you to provide a service you are not properly equipped to do.
- Your client asks you to provide a service you are not properly trained how to do.

These are all very good reasons to hire subcontractors. Hiring subs allows you to expand your service offerings and be a one-stop problem solver for your clients—without adding more employees. This is a good way to expand your business without adding risk. In fact, you can, and should, develop a very profitable business serving as a kind of general contractor for your clients.

Allow me to expand on the subject. The first subcontractor many landscape contractors hire is a professional pesticide applicator who specializes in turfgrass weed control and fertilization. After all, you can avoid the pesticide license requirement in many states if you hire a weed-and-feed lawn care sub.

Another frequent subcontractor is the arborist. As you recall, your insurance agent was "crystal clear" in explaining that your insurance policy says "no tree pruning more than fifteen feet off the ground." Once again, you have made a very good decision. Hire a specialist.

In your quest to provide your clients with a "one-stop shop" for everything landscaping related, you develop relationships with masons, electricians, plumbers, irrigation experts, carpenters, concrete contractors, and pool contractors. The list can go on and on. If you are designing the work you are selling, your imagination is the only thing holding you back from working with more new subs with new kinds of expertise. So look to hire subcontractors for the jobs you are not licensed, insured, equipped, or properly trained to do.

Then one day you realize you are giving away a ton of work to a subcontractor who may not share your values of timely, professional service. The little things start to add up: The project schedule is delayed because the subcontractors didn't show up on the day they promised, or there is some part of their work that must be corrected after the job has been completed and you're having a struggle getting them to return for the warranty repair. With each of these situations, you contemplate how to correct the problem for the next job. Should you

- better train your existing subcontractor;
- find another subcontractor;
- or learn how to do the work yourself and bring this work in-house?

These are nearly the exact same questions we face as we hire employees. In just about every case, we don't write down clear definitions of what we expect from subcontractors. Many times we look at a subcontractor as one of our "kinfolk." We tell ourselves, "Our brother-in-contracting is a good guy. He will do what he promised because he is just like me, a contractor. We don't have to go through all the formality of written contracts, detailed plans, and defined payment schedules with our brother, do we?"

Absolutely, positively, yes. Every single time you hire subs, you'd better have a well-defined contract because you will be held responsible for their work. And since you may not be licensed or insured to do that work, you may be subject to audits that could lead to future expenses if the documents to protect your company are not in order. Permits, insurance certificates, and written contract specifications can be very expensive when not acquired during a subcontractor relationship.

If you encounter a subcontractor who gives you a verbal quote and no written proposal, don't hire him or her. The absence of paperwork is an absence of professionalism and a roadmap to future trouble.

Subs or Employees?

Now that we're talking about paperwork and administrative functions, it's appropriate to mention the dark side of hiring subcontractors within the landscape contracting industry. I see this in company after company, but most frequently in young companies with very little business experience.

The landscape business owner "heard from another contractor" that he could save some serious paperwork and avoid payroll taxes if he hires subs instead of employees. And so the debate begins. Is this person you pay a subcontractor or an employee? If you have yet to be audited, let me educate you.

Our friends over at the IRS care a great deal about how you pay people. In fact, they have a twenty-part test to determine if someone should be treated as an employee or a subcontractor. The heart of the matter comes down to control. Do the people you pay set their own schedules, follow their own rules, work with their own tools, work by the contract, and work for others beside you? If you answer no to even some of these questions, you likely have employees, not subcontractors in the IRS's eyes.

My advice is simply this: Building a successful business will require you to have well-trained people who follow your rules, work with your tools, and work your posted schedule. And, yes, you will always need subcontractors in your company. As Michael says, you want to develop subcontractor relationships that share your values and dedication of service to the client. Let's examine this topic a little bit further.

Working for landscape contractors as their consultant, advisor, or mentor in more than forty U.S. states and Canada, I have seen a huge variety of internal policies for hiring subcontractors. Some companies avoid the idea, rarely hiring subs, and yet others build their business with the same idea. Here are the most powerful reasons to hire a subcontractor:

- You develop key relationships with contractors who specialize in complementary work.
- You expand your service offerings.
- You gain confidence in offering more comprehensive landscape designs.
- You expand your capacity for work during peak seasons.
- You expand your geographical territory.
- You learn how to be an effective manager.

- And here is the big one: You learn that you can capitalize on your client relationships without having to do all the work in-house.

Pay careful attention to this next statement. It is completely ethical, legal, and morally acceptable to make money by hiring subcontractors. This comes as a surprise to those who have yet to really learn this business. But now you know!

Landscape contractors who develop strong customer relationships earn the right to serve the customer in a wide variety of ways. Today's busy homeowners, property managers, builders, or general contractors may not have the time or the inclination to develop an extensive list of specialty contractors to take care of their every need. This is where you will find profitable opportunities.

Ask and You Shall Receive!

Go back to the beginning of this chapter and look at the list of reasons that got you started hiring subcontractors in the first place. Notice the words at the beginning of each reason for hiring subs: "Your client asks you . . . ." It's time for you to reverse the role and ask the questions yourself.

You can position yourself as a problem solver by always asking your customer, "Is there anything else you need help with around here?" This is the most basic form of marketing and sales the world has ever seen. It's called "Find a Need and Fill It." If you are bold enough to ask this simple question of every client, you will never run out of work again.

One day, you may take inventory of your revenue and learn that you have added hundreds of thousands or millions of dollars to your sales. How? By serving your clients on a higher level and becoming a manager of subcontractors. Or, as I prefer to think of it, by becoming the problem solver for your clients.

If your firm is properly positioned as a problem solver in your client's mind, there is no limit to the amount of services you can offer, provide, manage, and profit from. You might shudder at the thought of hiring a roofer, plumber, electrician, chimney sweep, or any other subcontractor listed in this discussion. But the only reason you have not done it is you don't have a system for hiring, managing, and profiting from subcontractors.

I hope you will agree. You need clear, well-written documentation within your company. The reason for this is simple: You want to become a world-class company with world-class profits. Your subcontractor development plan will help you manage more effectively, a critical part of your strategy to grow profits. Increasing profits sound exciting to you? You bet it is. Now let's find out what Michael has to say about estimating your fees. ✤

CHAPTER 13

On the Subject of Estimating

Michael E. Gerber

The way a Chihuahua goes about eating a dead elephant is to take a bite and be very present with that bite. In spiritual growth, the definitive act is to take one step and let tomorrow's step take care of itself.
—William H. Houff, *Infinity in Your Hand: A Guide for the Spiritually Curious*

One of the greatest weaknesses of landscape contractors is accurately estimating how long appointments will take and then scheduling their clients accordingly. *Webster's Eleventh* defines estimate as "a rough or approximate calculation." Anyone who has visited a potential jobsite knows that those estimates can be rough indeed.

Do you want to see someone who gives you a rough approximation? What if your landscape contractor gave you a rough approximation of your garden's condition?

The fact is, we can predict many things we don't typically predict. For example, there are ways to learn the truth about people who come in complaining about dying plants or pest-ridden trees. Look at the steps of the process. Most of the things you do are standard, so develop a step-by-step system and stick to it.

In my book *The E-Myth Manager*, I raised eyebrows by suggesting that doctors eliminate the waiting room. Why? You don't need it if you're always on time. The same goes for a landscaping company. If you're always on time, then your clients don't have to wait. What if you were to eliminate design estimations from the process or not do them for free? Begin in the first phone call to set clients' expectations and their perception of value.

What if a landscape contractor made this promise: On time, every time, as promised, or we pay for it.

"Impossible!" landscape contractors cry. "Each client is different. We simply can't know how long each appointment will take."

Do you follow this? Since landscape contractors believe they're incapable of knowing how to organize their time, they build a business based on lack of knowing and lack of control. They build a business based on estimates.

I once had a landscape contractor ask me, "What happens when someone calls about a landscape design and you discover their property has a major drainage problem?"

This is your chance to demonstrate professionalism. Point out the problem, acknowledge the new opportunity to serve and stick to your meeting schedule. Provide your insight, offer creative ideas and build rapport.

The solution is interest, attention, analysis. Try detailing what you do at the beginning of an interaction, what you do in the middle, and what you do at the end. How long does each take? In the absence of such detailed, quantified standards, everything ends up being an estimate, and a poor estimate at that. What will it take to move clients one step closer to trusting you with this portion of the home improvement project?

However, a business organized around a system has time for proper attention. It's built right into the system.

Too many landscape contractors have grown accustomed to thinking in terms of estimates without thinking about what the term really means. Is it any wonder many landscaping companies are in trouble?

Enlightened landscape contractors, in contrast, banish the word *estimate* from their vocabulary. When it comes to estimating, just say no!

"But you can never be exact," landscape contractors have told me for years. "Close, maybe. But never exact."

I have a simple answer to that: *You have to be.* You simply can't afford to be inexact. You can't accept inexactness in yourself or in your landscaping company.

You can't go to work every day believing that your company, the work you do, and the commitments you make are all too complex and unpredictable to be exact. With a mindset like that, you're doomed to run a sloppy ship—a ship that will eventually sink and suck you down with it!

This is so easy to avoid. Sloppiness—in both thought and action—is the root cause of your frustrations.

The solution to those frustrations is clarity. Clarity gives you the ability to set a clear direction, which fuels the momentum you need to grow your business.

Clarity, direction, momentum—they all come from insisting on exactness.

But how do you create exactness in a hopelessly inexact world? The answer is this: You discover the exactness in your practice by refusing to do any work that can't be controlled exactly.

The only other option is to analyze the market, determine where the opportunities are, and then organize your company to be the exact provider of the services you've chosen to offer.

Two choices, and only two choices: (1) Evaluate your company and then limit yourself to the tasks you know you can do exactly, or (2) start all over by analyzing the market, identifying the key opportunities in that market, and building a company that operates exactly.

What you cannot do, what you must refuse to do, from this day forward, is to allow yourself to operate with an inexact mindset. It will lead you to ruin.

Which leads us inexorably back to the word I have been using through this book: *systems*.

Who makes estimates? Only landscape contractors who are unclear about exactly how to do the task in question. Only landscape contractors whose experience has taught them that if something can go wrong, it will—and to them!

I'm not suggesting that a *systems solution* will guarantee that you always perform exactly as promised. But I am saying that a systems solution will faithfully alert you when you're going off track, and will do it before you have to pay the price for it.

In short, with a systems solution in place, your need to estimate will be a thing of the past, both because you have organized your company to anticipate mistakes, and because you have put into place the system to do something about those mistakes before they blow up.

There's this too: To make a promise you intend to keep places a burden on you and your managers to dig deeply into how you intend to keep it. Such a burden will transform your intentions and increase your attention to detail.

With your promise comes dedication. With dedication comes integrity. With integrity comes consistency. With consistency comes results you can count on. And results you can count on mean that you get exactly what you hoped for at the outset of your company: the true pride of ownership that every landscape contractor should experience.

This brings us to the subject of *clients*. Who are they? Why do they come to you? How can you identify yours? And who *should* your clients be? But first let's see what Tony has to say about estimating. ✤

14

Estimating – Your Financial Future Looks Brighter

Tony Bass

Take care of the minutes and the hours will take care of themselves.
                                                                —Lord Chesterfield

T he reason most landscaping companies don't work is because they don't make enough money. The reason they don't make enough money is that most don't know how to correctly estimate their jobs. One day you're charging too much and losing jobs. The next day you're not charging enough and winning jobs. For one customer the price is this and for another customer the price is that. Lack of consistency kills you.

Shortly after reading *The E-Myth* and taking a six-month sabbatical to reinvent my landscaping business, I conducted an experiment within my own firm. I suggest you conduct a similar test inside your firm.

At the time, we had three people on my team who were pricing work. The assignment was simple. We allocated half of a day to bid on a project. We would all walk the property with the prospect at the same time, listen to the job requirements together, and then prepare our estimates independent of each other. In effect, we were bidding inside our own company.

It was important that we set a time limit within this exercise. Often, our prospects set time limits on us. Further, we had already learned that there was a direct correlation between providing quotes quickly and selling more work. So we agreed that we would meet the client at eight o'clock in the morning and have the estimate returned by noon.

The project was a commercial lawn maintenance opportunity. The property manager walked the property, showed us the property boundaries, and discussed the critical areas of the landscape that made an impact on curb appeal. The prospect simply told us what he was looking for. He did not provide a written set of guidelines. The prospect offered little information about why he had called us. The property was in pretty good condition. The only thing we could get out of the manager was, "You guys came highly recommended."

We asked questions about preferences for days of service, frequency of service, mulch services, floriculture services, irrigation services, and turf management. We verified the requirements regarding parking lot maintenance, access to the dumpster, and patio and breezeway maintenance.

Each of us took our own notes that day. Each of us used our experience, doing this type of work, to estimate the price for this job. We agreed to meet at eleven o'clock and compare our estimates.

At eleven o'clock, my fears were confirmed. I learned that my company had absolutely no way to consistently estimate the costs of one simple project. There was a 25 percent variance on price within my own firm. Which was the right price? Who knows?

We discussed our reasons for the prices we came up with, but the results were clear. The price from our firm was dependent on the estimator and not the company. And here is the most confusing part of the test. We all used the same man-hour rates and vendor material pricing. How could we start with the same information on pricing, visit the same property, collect the same site information, and arrive at three completely different prices?

In the words of Yoda, the Jedi Master, "Confused I am."

As I contemplated what I had just learned, I remembered getting an invitation from a vendor to a seminar entitled "Estimating and Bidding." In fact, the vendor had already paid my tuition if I would just show up. So I went to the "Estimating and Bidding" seminar.

Estimating – The Essential Skill for Contractors

Once again, I did not know what I did not know. And this lack of knowledge was costing me thousands of dollars each year. Ignorance is not stupidity. Ignorance is an absence of education. Ignorance is very expensive.

First, we lost bids by overpricing work. Overpricing work was not that painful, I thought. I did not actually lose money on jobs that I did not win. However, I lost a significant amount of time. Precious minutes, hours, and days were being squandered on estimating without winning bids.

Also, I had my feelings hurt by frequent rejection. "Your price is too high," the prospect would say. Or, "Tony, you better get that price right!"

So we worked on getting our price right. We would measure, design, measure again, shop materials, ask for discounts from vendors, and do it all over again the next day. I often wondered, *Why didn't I get this job? We poured our hearts and souls into this project.*

And then later I would ask, *Why in the world did I win this job?* Winning estimates that were priced too low was immensely painful. Based on what I learned at the estimating and bidding seminar, the problem was actually worse than I had ever imagined after our in-house estimating test. I did not have a system that accurately identified my underlying costs of doing business. Without clarity on underlying costs, I could never determine which jobs were losing money, which were making money, and which were breaking even.

After two hours in the estimating and bidding seminar, I knew I needed a new estimating system. There comes a time in every landscape contractor's life when he gets fed up. The landscape technician that can produce stunning results in the landscape can't necessarily produce stunning results on her financial statement. This becomes crystal clear when you sit with the banker, show the banker your financial statements, and ask to borrow money. I call this a "moment of truth" in business.

Your "moment of truth" is made up of countless hours of hard work. Your "moment of truth" is made up of all the jobs estimated and completed for the period. Your "moment of truth" is found on one financial report called your profit and loss statement—a financial snapshot of your year. Your banker will always judge your current success from this report. And this report is simply a summary of your ability to estimate correctly, manage correctly, sell correctly, and create money from your efforts. Complicated?

Do you enjoy showing your financial statements to your banker? You will if you have a nice, healthy profit.

Do you enjoy writing estimates? You will if you are able to get a majority of prospects to say, "You're hired."

Do you enjoy managing people? You will if you have a system that keeps score on productivity and profitability.

Do you enjoy sales? You will if you have a process that wins contracts without being the lowest bidder.

Do you enjoy sitting in the office and crunching numbers? You will if you know which numbers to crunch and what each number means in relation to your ability to make a predictable profit.

You need a financial system that ties together systems inside your landscape company like a rotating wheel. The wheel keeps rolling and rolling as time moves forward. Remember the wagon trains and horse-drawn buggies of the past? Our forefathers used this equipment to move from the East and tame the West. Picture the wooden wagon wheels in your mind. Each spoke in the wheel provided strength to the entire wheel. If one spoke was broken, the wheel would not function correctly. Your company is like that wagon wheel. Each step in the process of getting work must function correctly or your business will not function correctly.

In fact, your ability to make the transition from a landscape technician to a landscape business owner to a landscape entrepreneur is totally dependent on your ability to master the six skills of estimating:

1. Budgeting
2. Overhead recovery
3. Estimating
4. Bidding
5. Sales
6. Job costing

The interdependency of these skills is illustrated below. Master them and you can expand your reach further and further. When the price is right, you win in business.

Landscape Profit Wheel

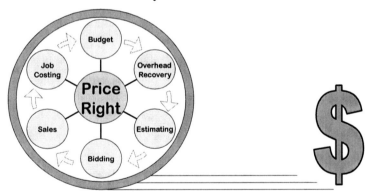

Perhaps you are having trouble understanding the true value of this wheel. The quest for making money is dependent on your personal ability to implement a turnkey system within each part of the financial wheel. You might have skipped, omitted, or fouled up one or more of these important financial processes.

If you have made the transition from landscape technician to landscape business owner, you have begun to master some parts of the financial wheel. To master them all, you have to build a system that works without your personal involvement.

If you have made the transition from landscape business owner to landscape entrepreneur, you have people working within every position of the wheel. Each person (or department) is focused on making his or her part of the wheel as strong as possible. About 3 percent of companies in our landscape industry have achieved this goal. Ninety-seven percent have not.

In my opinion, this is the most critical problem to solve in small business today. Get your pricing right before you try to grow.

Let's explore the six spokes on the Landscape Profit Wheel, starting with the Price Right Process.

Budgeting

Do you prepare a written financial budget? This is where business success, estimating, and control of your financial future all start. But you likely don't build an accurate budget.

Budgeting begins by sitting at a table with a list of questions. How much money will you spend in the thirty-three categories of overhead expenses? The answers are found within the 133 subcategories of spending decisions you will face over the next year. Your budget is crafted as you put the puzzle together one answered question at a time. This list of overhead questions is exhaustive, but the list is not infinite. From start to finish, without even using a special computer program, the process takes less than eight hours. With the right software, you can do it in half the time.

The art of building a budget is a skill anyone can learn. Just like the pilot of a jumbo jet, the right checklist will allow you to get the plane off the ground safely. Overhead can be budgeted, forecasted, and planned. By reviewing past spending records, projecting future business needs, and creating an action plan for the next twelve months, you can build an accurate budget for the company. When you build a well-thought-out budget, accurately plan for overhead expenses, and set a realistic profit goal, you have one spoke on the Landscape Profit Wheel in place.

Overhead Recovery

Once you know how much it will cost to operate your firm for a year, you must recover those costs as you estimate your jobs. Overhead recovery is simply the process you choose to mark up the direct costs to provide a service or produce the products. If you are not satisfied with the amount of money you earn, the benefits package your company provides, the vehicle you drive, the management team you employ, or the amount of education you have access to each year, you do not have an overhead recovery system. The science of overhead recovery methods is an ongoing debate, but here are the facts:

- If you fail to build a budget, you will never understand what your overhead costs are, exactly how much overhead there is to recover, or how to mark up your jobs in such a way to recover it.
- Every company has a unique overhead expense.
- Landscape technicians, start-up firms, and small owner-operator firms tend to underestimate their overhead.
- Overhead costs must be recovered before a dollar of profit is made.
- Overhead changes from year to year in every company and month to month in growing companies.

Estimating

Unlike overhead recovery, estimating can be an exact science. Estimating begins when you listen to prospects or clients and write down what they ask for, and it progresses when you prepare a set of plans. It continues and evolves when you provide written specifications. Estimating continues when you talk with vendors, subcontractors, equipment suppliers, and employees about how they may approach a given job.

Estimating mistakes kill you. The Landscape Profit Wheel can break faster through estimating mistakes than in any of the other five processes. Let's discuss the science of estimating.

As an estimator, you must predict the future. You begin with a set of plans. The degree to which you plan this future project in your mind will determine the estimate's accuracy. Skyscrapers are built with this method of estimating. Simply ask yourself, "What will I do the very first minute of the very first hour of the very first day of this project? What comes after that? What comes after that? What should I do next? What comes after that?" Document every step of the job. The estimate becomes a roadmap for the field worker.

You probably are not investing enough time in creating an accurate estimate. You feel hurried and start to guess. Sometimes you want to get the price in the prospect's hand and move on to the next opportunity. This kills you. This is why you have trouble making promises, like Michael E. Gerber explained.

What's so hard about estimating? There are four major components of direct costs in contracting: materials, subcontractors, equipment, and labor. Estimating materials cost is the easy part of estimating. If you can't accurately figure the costs on a materials list, get out of contracting immediately.

If you have clearly written specifications and plans, you should be able to accurately estimate materials costs. The absence of clearly-written plans and specifications leads to problems estimating materials. Failure to invest in a measuring wheel, then using the measuring wheel on each project to verify plans or site measurements, leads to inaccurate materials calculations. There are a number of reasons why you might miscalculate materials, but most can be avoided by investing more time in estimating.

Estimating subcontractor costs is even easier than calculating materials. You build relationships with reputable subs, you call them to look at your project, you provide written specifications, they provide a written quote, and you use their numbers to help calculate your costs of the project. Using subs expands your reach and lowers your risks in landscape contracting.

Estimating equipment costs for a job is where the stakes get a little higher. Your ability to lower costs for your prospects and clients is directly tied to your ability to use productivity-enhancing equipment in your company. Without equipment, you are forced to produce work from labor alone. And labor is where you incur the greatest risk in estimating.

Very few companies fail in landscape contracting because they missed an estimate due to incorrect materials and subcontractor cost estimates. However, many companies have experienced the pain of underestimating the amount of labor or equipment required for a project.

Accurate estimating is possible when you use a *production rate-based estimating system*. For every piece of equipment you own, you must know how much work it can produce in an hour. With accurate field measurements, knowledge of site conditions, and production rates, you can correctly estimate equipment and labor costs.

Here are a few examples of production rates for common landscape equipment.

Description	High	Average	Low	Notes
72" ZTR Mower	3.5 acres/hr.	3 acres/hr.	2.5 acres/hr.	
60" ZTR Mower	2.5 acres/hr.	2.25 acres/hr.	2.0 acres/hr.	
48" hydro-walk behind mower	1.5 acres/hr.	1.25 acres/hr.	1.0 acres/hr.	Slopes & ditches use low rate
Edging w/stick edger	4,500 linear feet/hr.	3,500 linear feet/hr.	2,500 linear feet/hr.	
Trencher — walk behind	100 linear feet/hr.	80 linear feet/hr.	60 linear feet/hr.	4" wide x 12" deep
Mini skid loader with trencher	200 linear feet/hr.	160 linear feet/hr.	120 linear feet/hr.	6" wide x 12" deep
Mini skid loader with 4" wide tiller	1,500 sq. feet/hr.	1,200 sq. feet/hr.	900 sq. feet/hr.	Till 6" depth

This equipment production rate list could continue for pages. Make a list of every piece of equipment you own. Then conduct time and motion studies on a variety of job sites to determine production rates. Variables in job site conditions are accounted for within the high-average-low range of production rates. With this information, you can estimate accurately.

You will need a similar list for labor-related tasks. Activities such as planting trees, shrubs, and sod can have a mixture of equipment and hand labor. Processes such as installing a paver patio require a series of labor- and equipment-driven steps. The amount of time required fertilizing, aerating, or overseeding a lawn can be predicted to the minute when you measure the property accurately and use a production rate-estimating method. Without production rates, you are always guessing the equipment and labor requirements for a job.

I have one contractor client who hired a statistician to work at his company for one year. The doctoral student stayed on job sites but never picked up a shovel or drove a piece of equipment. He was equipped with a stopwatch and a list of activities to measure. After one year, he had produced a production rate schedule more than two hundred pages long. This firm captured data for equipment and labor processes with unbelievable detail, which it now uses to accurately estimate jobs that have seemingly unlimited variables.

The risk in estimating and running your entire landscaping company is tied directly to correctly predicting the labor requirements to complete a given job. This risk can be controlled with a step-by-step process. Remember, you must have systems in your firm that can be duplicated and replicated as people come and go. And you don't have to do all the estimating yourself if you have a system. The absence of a production rate-estimating system flattens your Landscape Profit Wheel forever.

Bidding

Bidding is not a science. It is an art. Bidding is turning in a number. Bidding alone does not make you money, but winning bids can. Losing bids can prevent you from losing money. It will always be the estimating process that protects you, prepares you, and supports you in the bidding process.

Government entities love the competitive bid process. The government official publicly states, "To get the best value for your tax dollar, we will have a competitive bid process. We will invite a number of qualified contractors and see who gives us the best bid." And, in many cases, they accept the lowest qualified bid. When bidding public work, your estimating better be exact, or you will never even compete.

The art of bidding is really the art of knowing what you are good at, perfecting your process, and doing the whole process again. There are countless contractors who have gotten so good at bidding that they are almost unbeatable. These guys are specialists. They have honed their bidding skills to an art form by delivering great prices to the public and the private sector.

Consider the frugal homeowner, the cost-conscience business owner, the thrifty non-profit agency manager, or the penny-wise project manager. They all seek low bids, right? Not so fast.

Go ask your biggest clients why they hired your firm. You can learn a lot. In many cases, they will tell you they want great value. They will tell you they want dependable services. They will let you know they treasure your expertise, advice, and personal attention. *They will tell you it's the little things you do that matter the most.* And yes, they will tell you they want a competitive price. They don't want to spend too much. No one wants to spend more money than they have to.

However, it is your responsibility to help your clients spend as much as they need to accomplish their landscape goals. Bidding can get your foot in the door. Once the door is opened, you must seize the opportunity to keep your Landscape Profit Wheel moving forward. Successful firms bid a lot of work. But they don't stop after turning in the bid.

The next spoke on the wheel of profit is where company after company can distinguish itself from the crowded marketplace.

Sales

Nothing happens until a sale is made. Sales professionals know this. Without sales, there is no landscape technician, no landscape business manager, and no entrepreneur who operates a landscape enterprise. Your firm will struggle if you always must be the low bidder to get work. Your ability to win bids without being the low bidder is tied directly to your ability to build a turnkey sales process.

Want to earn more money? To keep the Landscape Profit Wheel turning, you must build a sales team. To successfully build a sales team, you must build a sales process. Prospects always think your price is too high—this is not going to change. No matter how many years you stay in this business, your customers will always think they could get it done cheaper. And they are right.

There is always a startup firm with very little overhead or very little knowledge of overhead that could work for less money than your firm. There is always a bigger company with superior equipment, management, and resources that could knock on the door to your biggest client and say, "Give us a chance to save you some money." And guess what, your customer will listen to them.

You might not like the word *sales*. Maybe you don't think of yourself as a sales professional. Perhaps you prefer titles like designer, landscape consultant, landscape architect, project engineer, project manager, business developer, manager, gardener, or owner. Call yourself whatever you want, but if you fail to convert leads into prospects, prospects into customers, and customers into clients, your company will fail. The Landscape Profit Wheel will break.

This topic is so important for your future that Michael and I have dedicated our next few chapters to a discussion of the sales process and how to interact with your prospects, customers, and clients more in depth.

Job Costing

To complete the circle on the Landscape Profit Wheel, you must seek continuous improvement in your estimating process. This happens within the job costing process. Job costing is the process of comparing your estimate to the actual costs *during* and *after* completing your jobs. Each time you do this, you learn a valuable lesson. Job costing is the secret ingredient to profit. You earn more by learning more. In fact, job costing gives you the right to earn more than you have ever earned in the past.

Too often, landscape contractors get super busy in the spring. They bust their butts to hurry up and get to the next project. After all, there are so many opportunities to make more money. However, the money seems to disappear. You can help solve the mystery of disappearing profit by comparing estimated costs to actual costs. As you compare, you can improve your production rate data as described above. Then you will have greater profits as you continually improve the estimating process.

When you implement job costing as a daily process within your firm, everyone learns. The field worker, the estimator, the materials buyer, the manager, and the sales professional all get smarter.

Let me be clear here: Job costing is not simply checking your materials list of purchased products against your estimated list of materials. Job costing is not simply buying smarter. There is much more involved. Job costing will track materials cost, but it will track labor costs even more closely.

To be exact within your estimating process, you must precisely allocate, track, and measure your field labor's accomplishments in labor hours. The most profitable companies in our industry have the ability to allocate labor hours per project, specific to the crew, day, and hour. They share these predictions with their field team and the managers keep score by job costing. Day after day, week after week, and year after year, the firm produces profits while talking to the field about labor hours.

The firms that do this become super profit producers, nearly eliminating uncertainty. They produce the right price. The Landscape

Profit Wheel, as a system of interdependent systems, rewards the entrepreneur for being a business owner with a predictable return on his or her investment.

Making Promises

Are you prepared to make promises instead of writing estimates? Do you want to come up with the right price for your prospects and clients? You can with the Landscape Profit Wheel. You need strong systems as you roll down the bumpy contracting road. Every job is different, and every customer is different, but the process you follow adjusts subtly as you encounter bumps along the way.

Your moment of truth approaches. It happens each time you review your profit-and-loss statement. Are you satisfied with the income from your business? If you are not satisfied with the financial results of your company, it's because you are lacking specific knowledge. Better business decisions can be part of your brighter financial future.

You can become wealthy as a landscape contractor, I promise.

The information within these pages provides a glimpse into improving your potential.

Now let's find out what Michael has to say about clients. ✤

CHAPTER
15

On the Subject
of Clients

Michael E. Gerber

*Some clients I see are actually draining into their bodies the diseased
thoughts of their minds.*
—Zachary T. Bercovitz, *Wisdom for the Soul:
Five Millennia of Prescriptions for Spiritual Healing*

W hen it comes to the business of landscaping, the best definition of *clients* I've ever heard is this: very special people
who drive most landscape contractors crazy.

Does that work for you?

After all, clients rarely show any appreciation for what a landscape contractor has to go through to do the job as promised. Don't
they always think the price is too high? And don't they focus on
problems, broken promises, and the mistakes they think you make,
rather than all the ways you bend over backward to give them what
they need?

127

Do you ever hear other landscape contractors voice these complaints? More to the point, have you ever voiced them yourself? Well, you're not alone. I have yet to meet a landscape contractor who doesn't suffer from a strong case of client confusion.

Client confusion is about

- what your clients really want;
- how to communicate effectively with your clients;
- how to keep your clients truly happy;
- how to deal with client dissatisfaction; and
- whom to call client.

Confusion 1: What Your Clients Really Want

Your clients aren't just people, they're very specific kinds of people. Let me share with you the six categories of clients as seen from the E-Myth marketing perspective: (1) tactile clients, (2) neutral clients, (3) withdrawal clients, (4) experimental clients, (5) transitional clients, and (6) traditional clients.

Your entire marketing strategy must be based on which type of client you are dealing. Each of the six client types spends money on landscaping services for very different, and identifiable, reasons. These are:

- Tactile clients get their major gratification from interacting with other people.
- Neutral clients get their major gratification from interacting with inanimate objects (computers, cars, information).
- Withdrawal clients get their major gratification from interacting with ideas (thoughts, concepts, stories).
- Experimental clients rationalize their buying decisions by perceiving that what they bought is new, revolutionary, and innovative.
- Transitional clients rationalize their buying decisions by perceiving that what they bought is dependable and reliable.

- Traditional clients rationalize their buying decisions by perceiving that what they bought is cost-effective, a good deal, and worth the money.

In short:

If your clients are tactile, you have to emphasize the people of your business.

If your clients are neutral, you have to emphasize the technology of your business.

If your clients are withdrawal clients, you have to emphasize the idea of your business.

If your clients are experimental clients, you have to emphasize the uniqueness of your business.

If your clients are transitional, you have to emphasize the dependability of your business.

If your clients are traditional, you have to talk about the financial competitiveness of your business.

What your clients want is determined by who they are. Who they are is regularly demonstrated by what they do. Think about the clients with whom you do business. Ask yourself: In which of the categories would I place them? What do they do for a living?

If your client is a mechanical engineer, for example, it's probably safe to assume he's a neutral client. If another one of your clients is a cardiologist, she's probably tactile. Accountants tend to be traditional, and software engineers are often experimental.

Having an idea about into which categories your clients may fall is very helpful in figuring out what they want. Of course, there's no exact science to it, and human beings constantly defy stereotypes. So don't take my word for it. You'll want to make your own analysis of the clients you serve.

Confusion 2: How to Communicate Effectively with Your Clients

The next step in the client satisfaction process is to decide how to magnify the characteristics of your business that are most likely to appeal to your preferred category of client. That begins with what marketing people call your *positioning strategy*.

What do I mean by *positioning* your business? You position your business with words—a few well-chosen words to tell your clients exactly what they want to hear. In marketing lingo, those words are called your USP, or *unique selling proposition*.

For example, if you are targeting tactile clients (those who love people), your USP could be: "Leafy Green—We offer a lifetime guarantee on every perennial we install. No questions asked." If you are targeting experimental clients (those who love new, revolutionary things), your USP could be: "Green and Clean Landscaping, where living on the edge is a way of life!" In other words, when they choose to schedule an appointment with you, they can count on both your services and equipment to be on the cutting edge of the landscaping industry.

Is this starting to make sense? Do you see how the ordinary things most landscape contractors do to get clients can be done in a significantly more effective way?

Once you understand the essential principles of marketing the E-Myth way, the strategies by which you attract clients can make an enormous difference in your market share.

Confusion 3: How to Keep Your Clients Happy

Let's say you've overcome the first two confusions. Great. Now how do you keep your clients happy?

Very simple—just keep your promise! And make sure your clients *know* you kept your promise every step of the way.

In short, giving your clients what they think they want is the key to keeping your clients (or anyone else, for that matter) really happy.

If your clients need to interact with people (high touch, tactile), make certain they do.

If they need to interact with things (high tech, neutral), make certain they do.

If they need to interact with ideas (in their head, withdrawal), make certain they do.

And so forth.

At E-Myth, we call this your *client fulfillment system*. It's the step-by-step process by which you do the task you've contracted to do and deliver what you've promised—on time, every time.

But what happens when your clients are *not* happy? What happens when you've done everything I've mentioned here and your client is still dissatisfied?

Confusion 4: How to Deal with Client Dissatisfaction

If you have followed each step up to this point, client dissatisfaction will be rare. But it can and will still occur—people are people, and some people will always find a way to be dissatisfied with something. Here's what to do about it:

- Always listen to what your clients are saying. And never interrupt while they're saying it.

- After you're sure you've heard all of your client's complaint, make absolutely certain you understand what she said by phrasing a question such as: "Can I repeat what you've just told me, Ms. Harton, to make absolutely certain I understand you?"

- Secure your client's acknowledgment that you have heard her complaint accurately.

- Apologize for whatever your client thinks you did that dissatisfied her, even if you didn't do it!

- After your client has acknowledged your apology, ask her exactly what would make her happy.

- Repeat what your client told you would make her happy, and get her acknowledgment that you have heard correctly.

- If at all possible, give your client exactly what she has asked for.

You may be thinking, *But what if my client wants something totally impossible?* Don't worry. If you've followed my recommendations to the letter, what your client asks for will seldom seem unreasonable.

Confusion 5: Whom to Call Clients

At this stage, it's important to ask yourself some questions about the kind of clients you hope to attract to your company:

- With which types of clients would you most like to do business?
- Where do you see your real market opportunities?
- Whom would you like to work with, provide services to, and position your business for?

To what category of client are you most drawn? A tactile client for whom people are most important? A neutral client for whom the mechanics of how you do business is most important? An experimental client for whom cutting-edge innovation is important? A traditional client for whom low cost and certainty of delivery are absolutely essential?

Once you've defined your ideal clients, go after them. There's no reason you can't attract these types of people to your landscaping company and give them exactly what they want.

In short, *it's all up to you.* No mystery. No magic. Just a systematic process for shaping your business's future. But you must have the passion to pursue the process. And you must be absolutely clear about every aspect of it.

Until you know your clients as well as you know yourself.

Until all your complaints about clients are a thing of the past.

Until you accept the undeniable fact that client acquisition and client satisfaction are more science than art.

But unless you're willing to grow your business, you better not follow any of these recommendations. Because if you do what I'm suggesting, it's going to grow.

That brings us to the subject of growth. But first, find out what Tony has to say about clients. ✤

CHAPTER 16

Customers or Clients?

Tony Bass

The purpose of business is to create and keep a customer.
—Peter F. Drucker

L et's begin this discussion with a look at the subtle difference between a customer and a client. According to the Merriam-Webster dictionary, a customer is "one that purchases a commodity or service." A client is "one that is under the protection of another; dependent; a person who engages the professional advice or services of another."

Growing your business is a science. The science begins between your own ears. How you think about your relationship with the people who pay for your services can make a huge difference in your ability to

- sell services at higher prices;
- retain your customers for the life of your company;

- convince your clients to return again and again as you add services and solutions to their problems;
- convince your clients to accept your recommendations with limited objections; and
- accept customer feedback.

If you want to transform your company from a mere commodity provider of landscape services to a trusted supplier of landscape and outdoor solutions, then change your goal of adding customers to a new goal of establishing client relationships. That's right; don't even try to get customers. You want clients. You want your clients to be dependent on you, your firm, and your team of experts. You want your client's clients to be dependent on your firm and under your care and protection.

Face it—it's a crowded and competitive marketplace, regardless of where you live. The market is full of eager landscape service providers capable of doing what you do. To compete, you need to build systems that help you stand out from the crowd. How you do your work separates you from the crowd. And like Michael says, "It matters what you say, how you say it, and the order in which you say it."

The $100,000 Project Challenge

During my seminars, I ask for a show of hands of companies who have completed a single contract with a value over $100,000. Typically, about half the room will raise their hands. I then ask how many of them would like to learn how to be awarded their first $100,000 project or win many more $100,000 projects this year? Invariably, everyone sits up straight in their seats, raises their hands, and says yes!

I then say, "Okay, it looks like everyone would like to do $100,000 projects. Who in the room is a top-producing salesperson? Who is a really good salesperson? Please raise your hand." Invariably, only 10 to 20 percent of the room raises their hands. And in most cases, they are slow to raise their hands.

It happens the same way in every city I visit. It's amazing to me! People indicate they have a desire to win prestigious and profitable $100,000 projects, but only a handful feel they have top-producing salespeople worthy of the goal. And they are exactly right. Most contractors and their salespeople are not prepared for the opportunity to win the big jobs with big profits, prestige, and rewards.

The $100,000 project challenge goes like this:

Imagine for a moment that through the miracle of marketing we are able to identify every person in your service area planning to complete a $100,000 landscape, irrigation, hardscape, and outdoor improvement project within the next twelve months. Imagine we are able to attract and assemble that group downtown in the largest room in the convention center. Imagine that all people in the room have to sign a personal guarantee that they will, in fact, do this $100,000 project within the next twelve months. There are several hundred, perhaps even a few thousand, people in the room. Does this sound like an exciting opportunity?

The event organizer recognizes that the group of property owners, developers, property managers, facility engineers, architects, and lovers of everything landscape have a limited amount of time. They are all busy, successful people with a lot to do. To get their project off the ground, they have assembled to listen to the top three landscape firms in their market. The event organizer has carefully pre-screened each firm as a company capable of completing a $100,000 landscape project.

Each landscape company invited to the event is allocated two minutes to present to the crowded room. You can say whatever you want. But you are strictly limited to two minutes on stage. The great news is, if you do a great job, you are likely to fill your schedule for the entire year!

What will you say? Even more puzzling, what will your two competitors say?

After I present that description of the $100,000 project challenge, I say to those gathered, "I need three volunteers to participate in the $100,000 project challenge right now. Let me *see, where are those people who raised their hands a moment ago and identified themselves as top producers? Who is prepared, right now, to present your company in the most effective, compelling way possible? Who is prepared to participate and win the $100,000 project challenge?"*

In every city, the attendees begin to sink down in their chairs. The people who identified themselves as top producers sulk and look away from my stare. Only after some prodding can I find three contractors willing to stand up in a crowded room and speak before the audience about their business, their passion, and their purpose for being a landscape contractor.

The $100,000 project challenge happens every day to your company, but rarely does it happen before a crowd of people. It happens to your company one phone call, one initial site visit, one proposal presentation, or one follow-up sales call at a time.

Consider this: If you had one chance to make all your sales for the whole year in two minutes, would you bust your butt to prepare? If you had two minutes in front of the very best prospects in your market area, would you prepare to make sure that every word spoken would set you apart from the crowd?

The lack of a written script for such a sales situation—in fact, any sales situation—limits your organization's growth. Growth is limited by counting on the owner to complete all (or most) sales. Growth is limited because the owner's sales results can't be duplicated with a second, third, and forth salesperson. This must change.

Your New USP

Begin building your Unique Selling Proposition (USP) by conducting your own internal $100,000 project challenge. Allow each person in your company to stand before the team and give his or her pitch. The process is called *role playing*, and role playing is one of the most powerful training techniques known to man. Performing in front of an audience is an unforgettable experience. Everyone learns valuable lessons.

Try to answer these questions during your exercise: Why should someone do business with our firm? What makes us special or unique?

You will learn that most of your team is stuck on a few words. They will say things like, "We offer top quality" or "We have dependable services." Some will take it a step further and say, "We are licensed and insured." The landscape designers exclaim, "We provide the most functional and creative landscape solutions in town." The irrigation technicians proudly claim, "We do it right the first time and make every drop count." The administrative staff passionately responds, "It's our teamwork that makes us special." But don't take my word for it. Try it and find out for yourself.

Guess what? All of your competitors are saying the exact same thing. To stand out in a crowded and competitive marketplace, you must incorporate solutions to your clients' problems into your USP. You need to change the rules. And like Michael points out so clearly, your clients' various types of personalities or backgrounds will cause them to respond differently to your words. What could happen if you changed the rules in your marketplace?

The new rules for standing out in a crowded and competitive marketplace dictate that you need to develop a *new* USP. Let's call it your Ultimate Strategic Position (USP). Let's identify the top problems from the various client segments you serve, and let's build a specially-crafted message that addresses *their problems*. This is some of the most difficult, tedious, and delicate work your organization may ever face. I strongly suggest that you get a person trained in the science of marketing to assist you and your team with the process. Time is short and the stakes are high.

What are you doing to make the phone ring with opportunities? Today, you must have ten to twenty marketing initiatives that communicate your brand consistently, while clearly offering solutions to the prospect's problems. To stand out in a crowded marketplace, you will also have five, ten, or twenty separate ways to attract leads. The only way to stand out today is to repetitively bring your brand and your solutions to the moving parade of qualified prospects.

Oh, there is one more thing. Perhaps you overlooked this from my discussion so far. If you are to sustain your company, you must learn the language of online marketing and sales or your firm will likely die. More on this in a later chapter.

The Landscape Profit Wheel Rolls On

I introduced you to the Landscape Profit Wheel in our last chapter. Here is the illustration once more to refresh your memory.

Landscape Profit Wheel

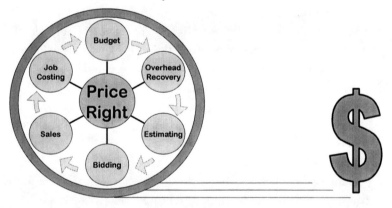

Within each spoke of the wheel is a system within a system. As the wheel moves forward with time, your organization learns how to improve. Each spoke on the wheel is dependent on the strength of the other spokes of wheel. Within each spoke of the wheel there are chances to improve profits. Feedback systems, like job costing, create the chance for continuous improvement. Let's look within the spoke titled *Sales* and see how this system within the system operates.

Creating Clients

The illustration above shows the six steps of the landscape sales process. Let's look at how to create clients in your landscape firm.

Marketing

Here are the basics. First, marketing *builds awareness* about your company, your products, and your services. Next, effective marketing *creates a perception of value* about your products and services. Third, the most effective marketing *creates a desire to purchase* from you and your company today. Every time you get the chance to write a check, invest time, or try a new way to attract clients, stop for a moment. Ask yourself if what you are doing will accomplish all three of these initiatives. If it does not, change it, enhance it, redesign it, or reconsider what you are about to do.

Do you want to grow? You can double the size of your company by adding one new marketing strategy per month in twelve to twenty-four months. Marketing is a science. It works. Most of you count on one, two, or perhaps three ways to generate leads. The firm that employs twelve unique marketing tools, one for each month of the year, will stand out in the marketplace. You can grow in almost any economy as you adjust your message to the season and your target audience. Conversely, you can choose a single marketing strategy and double your sales volume. Read on to learn how.

Lead Generation

I want your phone to ring non-stop every day of the week as a result of your marketing. You might think I am crazy but I say this based on my experience working as a consultant with more than two hundred landscape company owners. I say this based on conversations with another five hundred landscape company owners who have purchased products from my equipment companies.

Here is what I have heard time after time after time: "Tony, we rely on word of mouth for new business. We don't have time to answer the calls of a bunch of tire kickers." Each time I hear this from a business owner, I get a sick feeling in my stomach. Effective marketing targets your market and delivers a message that resonates with your ideal prospects. If you intend to survive, you must have a system to generate a never-ending flow of leads or your firm will die.

Word of mouth is the top source for sales for many contracting companies. But word of mouth alone did not make Coca-Cola the largest soft drink company in the world, and word of mouth alone will not grow your company much beyond the owner-operator size of the firm. Consider the strategy to target your market with laser beam-type focus.

The largest companies in this industry use this approach to grow. They simply conduct market research, identify the top prospects in the market, and go after them with sales professionals. The multi-million dollar producers focus their efforts on the top accounts. They go after these accounts until they get them. Their lead generation process is simple but overlooked by the vast majority of locally-owned landscape operations.

Think about it. What would happen if you targeted twenty, fifty, or one hundred prospects that had a $100,000 landscape budget per year? What if you developed a process to convert just 10 percent to

20 percent of these accounts? You can do the math. There is an easy path to $1 million in revenue. It matters what you say, how you say it, and the order in which you say it in. Does the $100,000 project challenge make more sense to you now?

Needs Analysis

A needs analysis system will effectively qualify or disqualify prospects so you don't view the attraction of leads and their requests for quotes as work without reward. With this tool, you can see massive lead generation as a necessary part of an effective sales machine. Make that phone ring, make the e-mail inbox fill up with inquiries, and collect endless prospect requests each time you visit the mailbox. This is the business's purpose, for crying out loud!

A well-scripted needs analysis process allows you to create the most effective marketing messages and then refines them to get better results over time. It is a series of carefully scripted questions to be asked in just the right order. The following sequence of questions has been proven successful time and time again in my business. They will qualify the best prospects for your firm when the market is expanding and opportunities are abundant. This market condition happens every spring when you have more opportunities for work than you can handle. So let's get in front of the best-qualified prospects. Try this series of questions and see improvement in the quality of your leads:

- Can you tell me more about your project?
- How did you find our company?
- What is your schedule?
- Who are the decision makers if questions should arise on the job?
- Can we make an appointment? (Determine if site plans or written specifications have been completed.)
- What is your budget? Can we confirm our appointment and initial goals?

At each step along the way you have the right to disqualify a prospect and to better qualify the prospect. By having a needs analysis system, your staff can improve the likelihood that a site visit is a good investment of your salesperson's time and talents. With an effective needs analysis system, you will qualify prospects up front in the initial conversation. This process is invaluable for those who serve residential and small commercial accounts.

Think about how this process will change if you have conducted market research and have prescreened the $100,000 projects. You would develop an incredible USP for your firm. First, you identify the most common complaints from interviews of similar demographic prospects. Second, you develop a short seminar on the top facility management problems and the most cost-effective solutions. Third, you call or stop by the target location with a simple message:

"Mr. Facility Manager, we are an environmental services firm that is providing an orientation for C-level business executives and facility managers titled, 'Seven Dangerous Trends in Facility Management that Bust Budgets and What Can Be Done to Lower Maintenance Costs.' My name is _____ with Mega Service Company, one of the top 150 facilities maintenance firms in the nation, and I will be in your area next week.

"I will discuss research during the orientation that has been underwritten by a top engineering firm and came to us and our partners at a cost of more than $100,000. We have identified your company as a likely firm to save 10 to 25 percent on maintenance costs this year by learning what is going on with today's top facilities managers.

"We have arranged to provide this research to your company at no cost or obligation for the next two weeks. The orientation will take about twenty to thirty minutes. I can bring coffee for a morning meeting or I can bring lunch for you and your team next Tuesday. Which would you prefer?"

Can you see how you can change the rules in the sales process? If you were a facility manager, chief financial officer (CFO), or chief executive officer (CEO) of a firm, would you want to hear what Mega

Service Company has to say? You better believe you would. C-level executives have a fiduciary responsibility to save money.

So now you know one way the big landscape companies grow, gain market share, and win the best contracts without always being the low bidder. They provide education to the well-qualified prospect.

Lead Conversion

You have a financial benchmark in your firm that defines your success in an amazing way. It does not show up on your financial statements. In fact, neither your accountant, nor your banker, nor the IRS will ever ask you for this financial benchmark. But if you and I work together, we are going to figure it out. I promise.

What I am talking about is your sales close ratio. The close ratio for your firm is a measurement of the effectiveness of the salesperson and the sales system. The calculation looks like this:

Number of contracts signed / Number of estimates written = Sales close ratio

Do you know your close ratio right now? Do you know this financial benchmark for each salesperson on your team? Can you identify this measurement for categories of prospects such as landscape installation versus lawn maintenance?

When you have the answers to these questions, you can measure success. I have worked with companies who are satisfied with a 10 percent close ratio. I have worked with firms who enjoy a close ratio in excess of 80 percent. In each case, the firm was looking for ways to improve. And in each case, they did improve by following the process outlined in the sales system you are reading about right now.

Lead conversion is about building trust with the prospect. You build trust with a series of small promises kept. Each phone call, each appointment, and each follow-up is a chance to build trust. It is incorrect to approach this business and the entire sales process with a bidder's mentality. A bidder focuses on providing a prospect a number. Call it a price, a quote, an estimate, a bid, or whatever you want. To escape this mentality, change the rules. Provide prospects solutions to their problems. I like what Michael suggests: Don't write estimates, make promises.

You should insist on providing written proposals in person to the decision makers identified. If you are a local service provider, make this a requirement of doing business. You join the group of commodity-rated service providers by providing price quotes via e-mail, fax, or mail, which can destroy the perceived value of your information. If you want to improve your close ratio, personal meetings are a surefire way to get it done. Get knee-to-knee with your prospects and invest time in educating them on a variety of options to meet their needs.

To separate yourself from the crowded marketplace, you need a system. Recognize this. If your marketing is effective enough to make your phone ring, you have a person who is interested in hiring a contractor. A prospect must have two pieces of information to hire a contractor: how much money they will spend and to whom to make the check out.

If you do enough work in the early portion of the sales process by building trust, the sale becomes a natural part of the relationship. Sales superstars talk about budgets early on in the conversation. They don't just write estimates, they learn what prospects want and what they can afford, and they build the proposal to give them what they want at a price they can afford. This way you can focus your efforts on making sure the check is written to your firm.

It's important to provide an adequate proposal that helps you stand out. If you focus on the price, in many cases you will make critical mistakes that cost you thousands of dollars each year in lost sales. You must make a strong case for why someone should hire your firm. The presentation process should include these features:

- A headline that uses the exact words from the original needs-assessment interview
- A personalized, short letter with an outline of the proposal materials
- Company history and resume
- Licenses, insurance, and references statement

- Company photograph of professional quality with your team and branded color scheme
- Certified workforce documentation
- Written project specifications explaining your work process in detail
- Materials list and/or project plans
- Price quote sheet with options
- The written warranty
- Credibility pieces (case studies, testimonials, photos, etc.)

You should be providing proposals that are ten to twelve pages long. Each page of the proposal guides the salesperson step-by-step through the presentation. Each subject needs to be discussed with the prospect to help your company win bids without being the lowest bidder. You want to build a perception of value before presenting the price, and demonstrate your attention to detail before working on the client's property. You can accomplish this with an organized lead-conversion process.

I hear the naysayers all the time. They say things like, "Tony, I can't produce a ten- to twelve-page proposal for a simple lawn maintenance estimate." Or I hear, "We don't have time to put that much effort into our small projects." In today's busy world I often hear, "I can't get a prospect to meet with me. They just ask me to e-mail them the price. People are too busy." And some others claim, "We prefer to drop off our quotes when the person is not at home."

To the naysayers, I respond, "I hope you enjoy low close ratios and providing a commodity service. Don't be surprised that you can't keep a contract beyond the initial term. Don't be surprised that you work for someone one time and never hear from him again. Don't be surprised that you spend a huge amount of time writing estimates but have trouble getting prospects to return your calls. These are the results for the landscape contractor who accepts being treated like a commodity."

The Mega Service Company that calls on the C-level executive and offers a turnkey landscape solution will never just e-mail or fax over a bid. If Mega Service Company is going to provide pricing, they will do their homework. They will insist on face-to-face meetings with all decision makers present, and they will close deals by working through objections encountered during those meetings.

You might be skeptical and say your company focuses on government contracts, and these bids are always based on being the lowest bidder.

Not so fast. Government contracts are often negotiated. Crafty government purchasing agents can choose to help a favored contractor write a creative proposal. (A "purchasing agent" is the buyer for government services.) The agent's goal is simple: Reduce the number of qualified bidders and allow their agency to choose a contractor based on factors other than the lowest bid. For example, the purchasing agent stipulates criteria very specific to their preferred contractor, such as that the contractor must be local, must have a certified workforce, and must be able to meet a narrow window for project completion or have a certain amount of experience.

Lead conversion is about being a professional salesperson. Building your sales system allows you to stand out in the crowded marketplace and win contracts without being the lowest bidder. It's time to keep your promises and provide the products and services contracted. Most landscape contractors do a good job in this area of the business. But good work alone will not convert a one-time customer to the loyal client who buys again and again. Let's discuss the final two steps to keeping your clients spending money with you year after year.

Billing

Your new sales process is converting customers to clients. Your company is growing, perhaps faster than you can keep up with. I don't want you to make mistakes that can ruin the relationship. In an attempt to get more work done, you delay some of the administrative work. In a haste to maintain cash flow, you send out invoices that are not accurate or not provided on a timely basis. Incorrect billing can quickly ruin your client relationship. Delayed billing makes it difficult to collect your money. Listen up.

The billing process is infinitely easier when you are making promises with written proposals. Billing is infinitely easier when you have an estimating system that predicts every expense in an organized manner. Billing is infinitely easier when you establish pricing in advance, follow a planned change-order process, and present the invoice promptly upon completion of the contract.

But here is a sad statistic.

Within the landscape contracting industry, we see half of one percent of invoices not paid in well-run companies. Depending on the type of clients you serve, uncollected invoices can quickly get out of hand and consume 5 percent of sales. You can prevent delayed payments, collection activities, and disputed invoices if you:

- make certain invoices match contracts prior to billing;
- present an invoice to the owner on the day of construction project walkthrough and job completion;
- have a change-order process that documents contract adjustments;
- invoice reoccurring maintenance services the same day of each month;
- generate detailed invoices to reinforce the details of your work;
- accept credit cards and online payments; and
- enforce a prompt collection process with all clients.

Your billing process is your first and best opportunity to reinforce your professionalism and begin your client retention efforts. I prefer to think of billing as a customer communication tool. The more often you are billing clients, the more often you are communicating with clients. Better communication will result in repeat business for the life of your firm. Let me explain.

Client Retention

We begin our efforts to retain clients for life with the customer feedback loop. Each invoice should provide an opportunity for the client to praise your firm or to complain. Praise for your firm, shared with your team, creates the ultimate employee motivation tool. Complaints addressed promptly create loyal clients.

What is a client feedback loop?

You can present three simple options. You can create a form, duplicate it online, or simply place the questions on the rear exterior of a return envelope for mailed payments. A simple client feedback loop will ask the client to choose one of the following options:

- I am pleased with my service.
- I am not pleased with my service, call me.
- Please contact me about a special project or service request.

What would happen in your firm if you asked every client these same three questions each month of the year? What if you asked these questions each time you provided a service? It would be like adding a new sales and customer service person to your organization. It will create opportunities for the most meaningful work you can ever do within your company.

When clients are pleased, you share the message with your team and build morale. When clients are not pleased, you correct the problem immediately and strengthen the relationship. When clients ask for special projects and services requests, you find ways to help them and enjoy close ratios of more than 80 percent.

This is how you transform a marginally profitable company into the elite profit-producing firm. When you have developed a true client relationship, you have earned a bond of trust. This bond of trust will lead to fewer price objections, larger projects, and repeat purchases.

The client retention process keeps the sales wheel of profits moving forward and accelerates your ability to learn how to better serve your clients, earn more money, and keep your people excited about working on your team.

I have seen this process turn eighteen-year-old landscape rookies into sales superstars and convert struggling landscape technicians into sales professionals. I have watched introverts become top producers with this system. And your team can improve as well.

I want to help you improve your potential. Avoid expensive mistakes in building your sales process. If you do what is described within this chapter, your business will grow. What will you do about that?

Now let's consider Michael's thoughts about growth. ✤

CHAPTER

17

On the Subject
of Growth

Michael E. Gerber

Growth is the only evidence of life.
—John Henry Newman, *Apologia Pro Vita Sua*

T he rule of business growth says that every business, like every
child, is destined to grow. Needs to grow. Is determined
to grow.

Once you've created your landscaping company, once you've
shaped the idea of it, the most natural thing for it to do is to . . . *grow!*
And if you stop it from growing, it will die.

Once a landscape contractor has started a business, it's his or
her job to help it grow. To nurture it and support it in every way. To
infuse it with these qualities:

- Purpose
- Passion
- Will

- Belief
- Personality
- Method

As your company grows, it naturally changes. And as it changes from a small company to something much bigger, you will begin to feel out of control. News flash: That's because you *are* out of control.

Your company *has* exceeded your know-how, sprinted right past you, and now it's taunting you to keep up. That leaves you two choices: Grow as big as your company demands you grow, or try to hold your company at its present level—at the level you feel most comfortable.

The sad fact is that most landscape contractors do the latter. They try to keep their company small, securely within their comfort zone. Doing what they know how to do, what they feel most comfortable doing. It's called playing it safe.

But as the company grows, the number, scale, and complexity of tasks will grow too until they threaten to overwhelm the landscape contractor. More people are needed. More space. More money. Everything seems to be happening at the same time. A hundred balls are in the air at once.

As I've said throughout this book: Most landscape contractors are not entrepreneurs. They aren't true businesspeople at all, but technicians suffering from an entrepreneurial seizure. Their philosophy of coping with the workload can be summarized as "just do it" rather than figuring out how to get it done through other people using innovative systems to produce consistent results.

Given most landscape contractors' inclination to be the master juggler in their companies, it's not surprising that as complexity increases, as work expands beyond their ability to do it, and as money becomes more elusive, they are just holding on, desperately juggling more and more balls. In the end, most collapse under the strain.

You can't expect your company to stand still. You can't expect your company to stay small. A company that stays small and depends on you to do everything isn't a company—it's a job!

Yes, just like your children, your business must be allowed to grow, flourish, change, and become more than it is. In this way, it will match your vision. And you know all about vision, right? You better. It's what you do best!

Do you feel the excitement? You should. After all, you know what your company is but not what it *can be*.

It's either going to grow or die. The choice is yours, but it is a choice that must be made. If you sit back and wait for change to overtake you, you will always have to answer no to this question: Are you ready?

That brings us to the subject of *change*. But first, let's see what Tony has to say about growth. ✤

18

Your
Growth

Tony Bass

Without continual growth and progress, such words as improvement, achievement, *and* success *have no meaning.*

—Benjamin Franklin

Michael E. Gerber says growth is the most natural thing a business can do. But growth requires some rather uncomfortable decisions for contractors who have been doing it, doing it, doing it for so long. For example, to grow, you need to take more vacations and work fewer hours. To grow, you need to strictly limit weekend work. To grow, you must get some new voices into your life. Let me explain.

I was speaking to a room full of professional landscape contractors when I introduced the concept of taking more vacations to facilitate growth. I had just explained to the class of about seventy-five attendees that I scheduled eight weeks of vacation each year for myself. I, the president of a multi-million dollar landscaping company, would take off one week about every six weeks of the year. I will never forget the reaction I got from two of my students.

First, a lady named Judy raised her hand and said, "My husband and I have been working on growing our business. We added employees and now we can't take any time off. In fact, we haven't taken a vacation in nearly five years. Our business will fall apart if we are not there."

I responded, "Judy, you are incapable of staying focused on the important work of life and business without time away. After five years without a vacation, you may have forgotten what happens. You see, each time you get ready to go on vacation, you have to work really hard and really fast to get ready to go away. Then, when you return, you have to work really hard and really fast to catch up. By taking time off, you actually force yourself to ignore unimportant work, and focus on the most important work. You actually gain personal productivity just before and just after each vacation. You get more done by taking vacations!"

I could see in her face a growing sense of disbelief. She said, "You don't understand. Our employees are incapable of surviving a week without us there to make decisions!"

About that time, another lady sitting at the same table spoke up. "Judy, why don't you go on a vacation and give us a chance to show you we can do it without you?"

There was utter silence in the room. The owner of the company, with an employee at her side, had just announced publicly that she did not believe her employees were capable of making the landscape company work for even one week without owner supervision.

It was a very uncomfortable moment for these two attendees. So I said, "Judy, whatever you believe, it will happen. Personally, as a business owner, I believe that I deserve and need eight weeks of vacation time each year. So I order my life to accomplish this goal. If you believe that you can't take a vacation, this becomes your reality. It's your choice.

"But my recommendation is that you take a vacation immediately. And you must take your husband with you. And you can't call the office even once while you are away. Not once. Don't do it!

Just see what happens. You are addicted to thinking you are needed. You are addicted to the urgent. You may feel like a drug addict being weaned from a sick habit the first three days away. But taking a vacation is critical to your ability to change and grow."

I have met dozens of "Judy" characters in my travels. Asleep and stuck in a rut. They are not even aware of how bad their situations have become.

I was back in the same city a year later to give a keynote address to almost two hundred landscape contractors when a lady came rushing up to me and said, "Tony, you changed my life last year here at this event. You encouraged my husband and me to take a vacation. I am proud to report that we took two weeks off this past year. We did not even realize how badly we needed the break. You were right. The business did not fall apart while we were away. Thank you for your advice."

I looked at her name badge. *Judy*.

Can you relate to this story? How do you feel about the concept of growth? Does the idea make you uncomfortable? Here is what I say. Growth in your company can give you more freedom and comfort in life. But sometimes you struggle because you're simply stuck. Getting new voices in your life can help you get unstuck.

Listen to this voice. Listen to my voice right now. You started this landscaping company with a dream. You use the dream to create a vision. You use this vision to establish your purpose. Your purpose becomes your mission. And growth is where you will find new challenges. Growth is where you will find your life. Solving new challenges forces you to grow personally and professionally, and keeps life interesting. This is what life is all about. Provide yourself, your team, and your clients the opportunity to grow, and your life has purpose. Staying the same is simply a slow death.

Can you grow? You already have. But you are far from finished growing. Just by reading these words, you are growing further and getting ready for the changes ahead. You have a new voice in your life, and your life as a landscape contractor will never be the same.

In the next chapter, Michael shares his thoughts about change. ❖

On the Subject
of Change

Michael E. Gerber

There is nothing permanent except change.
—Heraclitus of Ephesus, *Lives of the Philosophers*

S o your company is growing. That means, of course, that it's also changing. Which means it's driving you and everyone in your life crazy.

That's because, to most people, change is a diabolical thing. Tell most people they've got to change, and their first instinct is to crawl directly into a hole. Nothing threatens their existence more than change. Nothing cements their resistance more than change. Nothing!

Yet for the past thirty-five years, that's exactly what I've been proposing to small business owners: the need to change. Not for the sake of change itself, but for the sake of their lives.

I've talked to countless landscape contractors whose hopes weren't being realized through their company, whose lives were consumed by work, who slaved increasingly longer hours for decreasing pay, whose dissatisfaction grew as their enjoyment shriveled, whose company had become the worst job in the world, whose money was out of control, and whose employees were a source of never-ending hassles, just like their clients, their bank, and, increasingly, even their family.

More and more, these landscape contractors spent their time alone, dreading the unknown and anxious about the future. And even when they were with people, they didn't know how to relax. Their minds were always on the job. They were distracted by work, by the thought of work. By the fear of falling behind.

And yet, when confronted with their condition and offered an alternative, most of the same landscape contractors strenuously resisted it. They assumed that if there were a better way of doing business, they already would have figured it out. They derived comfort from knowing what they believed they already knew. They accepted the limitations of being a landscape contractor, the truth about people, or the limitations of what they could expect from their clients, their employees, their landscape subcontractors, their bankers—even their family and friends.

In short, most landscape contractors I've met over the years would rather live with the frustrations they already have than risk enduring new frustrations.

Isn't that true of most people you know? Rather than opening up to the infinite number of possibilities life offers, they prefer to bind their lives at respectable limits. After all, isn't that the most reasonable way to live?

I think not. I think we must learn to let go. I think that if you fail to embrace change, it will inevitably destroy you.

Conversely, by opening yourself to change, you give your landscaping company the opportunity to get the most from your talents.

Let me share with you an original way to think about change, about life, about who we are and what we do. About the stunning notion of expansion and contraction.

Contraction vs. Expansion

"Our salvation," a wise man once said, "is to allow." That is, to be open, to let go of our beliefs, to change. Only then can we move from a point of view to a viewing point.

That wise man was Thaddeus Golas, the author of a small, powerful book titled *The Lazy Man's Guide to Enlightenment* (Seed Center, 1971).

Among the many inspirational things he had to say was this compelling idea:

"*The basic function of each being is expanding and contracting. Expanded beings are permeable; contracted beings are dense and impermeable. Therefore each of us, alone or in combination, may appear as space, energy, or mass, depending on the ratio of expansion to contraction chosen, and what kind of vibrations each of us expresses by alternating expansion and contraction. Each being controls his [or her] own vibrations.*"

In other words, Golas tells us that the entire mystery of life can be summed up in two words: *expansion* and *contraction*. He goes on to say:

"We experience expansion as awareness, comprehension, under-standing, or whatever we wish to call it.

"When we are completely expanded, we have a feeling of total awareness, of being one with all life.

"At that level we have no resistance to any vibrations or inter-actions of other beings. It is timeless bliss, with unlimited choice of consciousness, perception, and feeling.

"When a (human) being is totally contracted, he is a mass particle, completely imploded.

"To the degree that he is contracted, a being is unable to be in the same space with others, so the contraction is felt as fear, pain, uncon-sciousness, ignorance, hatred, evil, and a whole host of strange feelings.

"At an extreme (of contraction), (a human being) has the feeling of being completely insane, of resisting everyone and everything, of being unable to choose the content of his consciousness.

"Of course, these are just the feelings appropriate to mass vibration levels, and he can get out of them at any time by expanding, by letting go of all resistance to what he thinks, sees, or feels."

Stay with me here. Because what Golas says is profoundly important. When you're feeling oppressed, overwhelmed, or exhausted by more than you can control—*contracted*, as Golas puts it—you can change your state to one of expansion.

According to Golas, the more contracted we are, the more threatened we are by change; the more expanded we are, the more open we are to change.

In our most enlightened—that is, open—state, change is as welcome as non-change. Everything is perceived as a part of ourselves. There is no inside or outside. Everything is one thing. Our sense of isolation is transformed to a feeling of ease, of light, and of joyful relationship with everything.

As infants, we didn't even think of change in the same way, because we lived those first days in an unthreatened state. Insensitive to the threat of loss, most young children are only aware of *what is*. Change is simply another form of *what is*. Change just *is*.

However, when we are in our most contracted—that is, closed—state, change is the most extreme threat. If the known is what I have, then the unknown must be what threatens to take away what I have. Change, then, is the unknown. And the unknown is fear. It's like being between trapezes.

To the fearful, change is threatening *because things may get worse*.

To the hopeful, change is encouraging *because things may get better*.

To the confident, change is inspiring because the challenge exists to improve things.

If you are fearful, you see difficulties in every opportunity. If you are fear-free, you see opportunities in every difficulty.

Fear protects what I have from being taken away. But it also disconnects me from the rest of the world. In other words, fear keeps me separate and alone.

Here's the exciting part of Golas's message: With this new under-standing of contraction and expansion, we can become completely attuned to where we are at all times.

If I am afraid, suspicious, skeptical, and resistant, I am in a contracted state. If I am joyful, open, interested, and willing, I am in an expanded state. Just knowing this puts me on an expanded path. Always remembering this, Golas says, brings enlightenment, which opens me even more.

Such openness gives me the ability to freely access my options. And taking advantage of options is the best part of change. Just as there are infinite ways to greet a client, there are infinite ways to run your company. If you believe Thaddeus Golas, your most exciting option is to be open to all of them.

Because your life is lived on a continuum between the most contracted and most expanded—the most closed and most open—states, change is best understood as the movement from one to the other, and back again.

Most small business owners I've met see change as a thing in itself, as something that just happens to them. Most experience change as a threat. Whenever change shows up at the door, they quickly slam it. Many bolt the door and pile up the furniture. Some even run for their gun.

Few of them understand that change isn't a thing in itself, but rather the manifestation of many things. You might call it the revela-tion of all possibilities. Think of it as the ability at any moment to sacrifice what we are for what we could become.

Change can either challenge us or threaten us. It's our choice. Our attitude toward change can either pave the way to success or throw up a roadblock.

Change is where opportunity lives. Without change we would stay exactly as we are. The universe would be frozen still. Time would end.

At any given moment, we are somewhere on the path between a contracted and expanded state. Most of us are in the middle of the journey, neither totally closed nor totally open. According to Golas, change is our movement from one place in the middle toward one of the two ends.

Do you want to move toward contraction or toward enlightenment? Because without change, you are hopelessly stuck with what you've got.

Without change,

- we have no hope;
- we cannot know true joy;
- we will not get better; and
- we will continue to focus exclusively on what we have and the threat of losing it.

All of this negativity contracts us even more, until, at the extreme closed end of the spectrum, we become a black hole so dense that no light can escape.

Sadly, the harder we try to hold on to what we've got, the less able we are to do so. So we try still harder, which eventually drags us even deeper into the black hole of contraction.

Are you like that? Do you know anybody who is?

Think of change as the movement between where we are and where we're not. That leaves only two directions for change: either moving forward or slipping backward. We either become more contracted or more expanded.

The next step is to link change to how we feel. If we feel afraid, change is dragging us backward. If we feel open, change is pushing us forward.

Change is not a thing in itself, but a movement of our consciousness. By tuning in, by paying attention, we get clues to the state of our being.

Change, then, is not an outcome or something to be acquired. Change is a shift of our consciousness, of our being, of our humanity, of our attention, of our relationship with all other beings in the universe.

We are either "more in relationship" or "less in relationship." Change is the movement in either of those directions. The exciting part is that *we possess the ability to decide which way we go—and to know in the moment which way we're moving.*

Closed, open; open, closed. Two directions in the universe. The choice is yours.

Do you see the profound opportunity available to you? What an extraordinary way to live!

Enlightenment is not reserved for the sainted. Rather, it comes to us as we become more sensitive to ourselves. Eventually, we become our own guides, alerting ourselves to our state, moment by moment: *open . . . closed . . . open . . . closed.*

Listen to your inner voice, your ally, and feel what it's like to be open and closed. Experience the instant of choice in both directions.

You will feel the awareness growing. It may be only a flash at first, so be alert. This feeling is accessible, but only if you avoid the black hole of contraction.

Are you afraid that you're totally contracted? Don't be—it's doubtful. The fact that you're still reading this book suggests that you're moving in the opposite direction.

You're more like a running back seeking the open field. You can see the opportunity gleaming in the distance. In the open direction.

Understand that I'm not saying that change itself is a point on the path; rather, it's the all-important movement.

Change is *in you*, not *out there.*

What path are you on? The path of liberation? Or the path of crystallization?

As we know, change can be for the better or for the worse.

If change is happening *inside* of you, it is for the worse only if you remain closed to it. The key, then, is your attitude—your acceptance or rejection of change. Change can be for the better only if you accept it. And it will certainly be for the worse if you don't.

Remember, change is nothing in itself. Without you, change doesn't exist. Change is happening inside each of us, giving us clues to where we are at any point in time.

Rejoice in change, for it's a sign you are alive.

Are we open? Are we closed? If we're open, good things are bound to happen. If we're closed, things will only get worse.

According to Golas, it's as simple as that. Whatever happens defines where we are. *How* we are is *where* we are. It cannot be any other way.

For change is life.

Charles Darwin wrote, "It is not the strongest of the species that survive, nor the most intelligent, but the one that proves itself most responsive to change."

The growth of your landscaping company, then, is its change. Your role is to go with it, to be with it, to share the joy, embrace the opportunities, meet the challenges, and learn the lessons.

Remember, there are three kinds of people: (1) those who make things happen, (2) those who let things happen, and (3) those who wonder what the hell happened. The people who make things happen are masters of change. The other two are its victims.

Which type are you?

The Big Change

If all of this is going to mean anything to the life of your company, you have to know when you're going to leave it. At what point, in your company's rise from where it is now to where it can ultimately grow, are you going to sell it? Because if you don't have a clear picture of when you want out, your company is the master of your destiny, not the reverse.

As we said earlier, the most valuable form of money is equity, and unless your business vision includes your equity and how you will use it to your advantage, your company will forever consume you.

Your company is potentially the best friend you ever had. It is your company's nature to serve you, so let it. If, however, you are not a wise steward, if you do not tell your company what you expect from it, it will run rampant, abuse you, use you, and confuse you.

Change. Growth. Equity.

Focus on the point in the future when you will take leave of your company. Now reconsider your goals in that context. Be specific. Write them down.

Skipping this step is like tiptoeing through earthquake country. Who can say where the fault line is waiting? And who knows exactly when your whole world may come crashing down around you?

Which brings us to the subject of *time*. But first, let's see what Tony has to say regarding change. ❧

CHAPTER 20

Change with a Capital C

Tony Bass

You can't teach an old dog new tricks.

—An English proverb

I have a client who owns a multi-million dollar landscape contracting company. He hired me to work with him and his management team on improving the business. The process began with a thorough review of the pre-consultation questionnaire. Some of the challenging questions he had to answer in preparation for our meeting were, "How long do you expect your company to operate after you leave or die?" and "Who will operate it?"

His answers were amazing and a great example for all landscape contractors to consider. He gave me a detailed description of who would be in charge upon his death. His spouse would take over. There were further detailed instructions in the event that both he and his wife should pass away at the same time. This business owner was thoughtful. Much more so than most of the business owners with whom I have worked. He named a board of directors, made up of company outsiders to whom the management team would answer. I was impressed by his attention to detail. Then I asked him a question that stumped him. I would like for you to consider the same question: What is your exit strategy if you live?

This question takes you in a new direction with completely different challenges. I first read *The E-Myth* when I was twenty-seven years old. It was within those pages that Michael E. Gerber introduced me to the following idea: The only reason to start a business is to sell it one day.

Think about those words. Depending on where you are in your career, you may be open or closed to the concept. At twenty-seven years of age, I could not even comprehend the idea. However, Michael E. Gerber's words entered my mind and this new idea could not escape.

When will you leave your business? Will you leave after an illness, a serious injury, an economic downturn, or your largest contract is lost? Or could you plan your exit when the business is running at its best?

As I said before, I retired at forty-one years old, twenty-four years ahead of what the government recommends. This was time with a capital *T*, life with a capital *L*, and change with a capital *C*. Could you create a company that buys you twenty-four years of life? I am living proof that you can. But it's your choice.

Change with a Little c

If landscape entrepreneurs can't learn something new, and change with the times, they have outgrown their usefulness. Without acceptance of change, the free market renders their companies obsolete and those companies will die. Death is often the result of the owner not paying attention to change with a little *c*, or small, almost insignificant changes that shift the business, the industry, or client buying habits.

Busy, busy, busy business owners, asleep at the wheel, miss the small changes time and again. Then one day, this series of small changes leads to a big change—the company's demise. And they didn't unlock equity for themselves or their heirs. What a scary idea.

As I write this message, there are landscape firms that are dying and there are firms that are looking change in the face, embracing it with an open mind, and growing in spite of economic challenges.

Consider Judy's story from chapter 18. Until Judy had a new voice, she was closed to an idea that would allow her to grow. In my career I have experienced more than twenty little changes that completely altered the landscape industry forever. Countless small changes have occurred and untold changes are yet to come. I don't have room to discuss all the changes, so I will introduce you to three game changers. See how you are doing in these areas.

No More Steering Wheels

Take the lawn mower, for example. As an industry, we have witnessed the obsolescence of the garden tractor as a practical tool for the professional landscape maintenance contractor. Although you can purchase a garden tractor today for 25 percent of the cost of a hydraulically-steered, zero-turn riding mower, walk-behind mower, or stand-on mower, you wouldn't be caught dead with an outdated, belt drive, garden tractor. New mower technology increased personal productivity by four to six times the garden tractor. No more steering wheels.

Take the mini-skid loader. My company purchased one of the first fifty Dingo Digging machines sold in the United States. I will never forget looking at this little green machine sitting on a trade show floor for the first time. The landscape construction department manager had grabbed me by the arm and dragged me over to this booth to look at the machine. I gazed at the smallness of this machine, the arsenal of complementary attachments, and then begin to smirk. *You mean to tell me this little Tonka toy is going to improve my productivity?* I simply had to see it to believe it.

A few weeks later we had the machine on a job site testing it out for ourselves. Immediately, we doubled our productivity for trenching irrigation lines. Instantly, we improved the bed preparation process of tilling and leveling by a factor of three. We improved the tree planting process by a factor of two. Our cost for labor in delivery of landscaping services fell instantly. Our company quickly grew market share with the lower cost of doing business and lower prices for our clients. One small machine changed my company.

The competition was slow to adopt the technology. In fact, it was three years before a local competitor stepped up to the plate, invested in the new technology, and began to lower its prices.

Today, these machines are used in the majority of successful landscape firms across the landscape industry. The compact design allows for handwork to be eliminated or greatly reduced in tight spaces, resulting in lower costs in landscaping departments. A complete paradigm shift occurred on the process of landscape work. Less labor, more work. No steering wheel needed.

No More Trailers

Earlier in this book, I told you I took a six-month sabbatical to work *on* my landscaping business. I never could have guessed what would happen as I changed my work.

My sabbatical began with careful observation. This observation process is called a *time and motion study*. I had learned about the process in my agricultural engineering classes at the University of Georgia, but had yet to apply this knowledge in an intelligent way. I was too busy doing it, doing it, doing it, and working *in* the business. But this was different. I decided to change my work—this was working *on* the business.

This simple process has three phases: (1) observe the motion, (2) document how much time it takes, and (3) get creative on ways to reduce the time required to get the same or better results. Anyone can do it.

I began with the lawn maintenance crews. I watched and recorded the time required for every step the lawn maintenance crew took on a daily basis.

You can try this test for yourself. Take out one of your trucks with a big, bulky trailer hooked up behind it. Then get in another truck without a trailer and follow the first truck around town. You will quickly see the truck without a trailer moves up and down the roads a little faster. The truck with a trailer is always holding back the truck without a trailer from where it's going.

In NASCAR terms, the trailer is blocking. In each of our studies, we came back with the exact same conclusion. If we can eliminate the trailer, we can improve productivity right away. But how can we get all that equipment in the back of the truck and do away with a trailer?

Over a six-month period, I documented every single step involved when providing a landscape maintenance service visit for a client. From morning set-up, to arrival at the first job, to the return trip to the shop, I documented each step, accounting for even the smallest details. For example, how many footsteps do I take from the time clock to the parking lot where the trucks are located?

Minute-by-minute, hour-by-hour, day-by-day, I built a diary of activities. With each step involved, I asked myself, *Would my client like to pay us to do what we are doing right now?* If my answer was no, I went to work on being creative.

Then I asked myself how we could eliminate this step or greatly reduce the number of times we do it. And the answer would slowly appear. It's amazing how much one person can accomplish when he or she focuses on one issue with a creative mind and a blank piece of paper.

Taking six months away from customer service, work in the field, and writing estimates cleared my mind for truly creative thinking. I read and re-read *The E-Myth* along the way, finding answers and inspiration to improve my business.

In the fifth month I had a detailed business plan that included a completely new system for organizing tools, transporting equipment, managing inventory, and marketing the company. Call it the "business in the box," "the franchise prototype," "the streamlined business model," or whatever you want.

I also came up with the "secret sauce" for gaining a serious competitive advantage in the delivery of lawn maintenance services. As we rolled out the new technology, during a recession, company sales and productivity took off like never before.

Some would look at what we had created and think it's simple, obvious, and easy to duplicate. However, the people that count—officers at the US Patent Office—awarded Dad and I our first patent for our landscaping truck with a hydraulic-operated loading ramp and tool storage system.

I organized a new company named Super Lawn Trucks™, recruited investors, and chose a management team to roll out this invention to professional landscape contractors. The business plan stated, "This (SLT) product will become as common as the zero-turn lawn mower in the landscape industry."

Today, Super Lawn Trucks™ are operating in forty-two states and Canada. The discovery has become a breakthrough for the entire landscape industry. Thousands of landscape contractors benefit from my six-month sabbatical working on the business of landscaping. Are you willing to change? Are you willing to quickly adopt new technology or will you simply be stuck in the comfort of the familiar past?

Stand Out from the Crowd

The Super Lawn Trucks™ system has helped companies enhance their image, improve daily operations, and lower overall business costs for more than a decade. With this equipment, companies reduce their need for warehouse space and lower storage costs. They also eliminate trailers, reduce accidents, and lower insurance costs.

We have watched companies capitalize on brilliant billboard advertising and lower marketing costs. We have watched company after company get its tools organized and increase productivity. Just like the process to produce a hamburger at McDonald's works every time, the Super Lawn Trucks™ system works. My clients are open to change.

Can you pass this next test? Are you open to change? Go to your computer, open your browser, pull up a search engine such as Google or Yahoo, and type in "landscape contractor [your city and state]." For example: "landscape contractor Austin Texas." Google quickly delivers 346,000 results from which to choose for Austin. Try this for a small community and the search engine will provide hundreds of names. How can a prospect find you out of hundreds or thousands of records? How do you stand out from the crowd?

You might say, "Wait a minute, Tony! I get all my business by word of mouth. Our company has a history in our community. We work from referrals in our firm."

I say, "Great!" You can and should get most of your business from referrals. But do not ignore the facts of doing business in today's world. This is a time of rapid change.

According to Nielson-Online.com, "In 2009, 81 percent of consumers are going online first to find out more about a business."

The Pew Research Center's Internet and American Life Project has extensive data regarding Americans' Internet use. They have organized this research into demographic profiles based on age and income levels. Today they report that "88 percent of Americans with household incomes of $75,000 per year research products online."

In 2010, a *USA Today* "Snapshots" study on small business strategy revealed that "63 percent of consumers turn to the Internet first to find local business." Do you think this trend is getting stronger or weaker as time moves forward?

Bill Gates predicts phone books will not even be printed in just a few years from now. Does this matter to you and your firm? You have probably long abandoned the phone book. However, you might continue to meet with representatives and listen to their suggestions. Good idea. How people find you has changed. The idea behind the "yellow pages" is changing with the times—you need professional marketing help to get your name out to the public. Stick with me.

Here is a key point. If you are not online, your absence can disqualify you from business opportunities. If you are online, you have a tool to support all marketing activities, support your brand, and take control of your corporate communications. Today, the company without a well-crafted online marketing plan and professionally designed website is like a person who is illiterate. You might survive, but you sure will make it hard to thrive.

Are You Online?

When I ask contractors this question, most say yes. Having an e-mail account and a web page is simply not enough to really be online. From social media and online customer satisfaction reviews, to Global Positioning Satellites (GPS) that track vehicles and locate accounts, to finding, organizing, and delivering client data online, the Internet is rapidly changing landscape companies.

Are you going to contract and avoid this change? Or will you expand, learning new skills and extending your reach? I strongly suggest that you do the latter. You get the chance to live and learn. Get in the flow of forward progress or be prepared for your company to become a garden tractor, still hanging around, but with less relevance every year. It's your choice. Expansion or contraction? You can't stay the same because time with a capital *T* is always moving forward.

The successful landscape entrepreneur will learn to seek, embrace, and harness change for continuous improvement. Come change with me.

Now let's see what Michael has to say about time. ✤

CHAPTER 21

On the Subject of Time

Michael E. Gerber

Take time to deliberate; but when the time for action arrives, stop thinking and go in.

—Andrew Jackson

"I'm running out of time!" landscape contractors often lament. "I've got to learn how to manage my time more carefully!"

Of course, they see no real solution to this problem. They're just worrying the subject to death. Singing the landscape contractor's blues.

Some make a real effort to control time. Maybe they go to time management classes, or faithfully try to record their activities during every hour of the day.

But it's hopeless. Even when landscape contractors work harder, even when they keep precise records of their time, there's always a shortage of it. It's as if they're looking at a square clock in a round universe. Something doesn't fit. The result: The landscape contractor is constantly chasing work, money, life.

And the reason is simple. Landscape contractors don't see time for what it really is. They think of time with a small *t*, rather than Time with a capital *T*.

Yet, Time is simply another word for *your life*. It's your ultimate asset, your gift at birth—and you can spend it any way you want. Do you know how you want to spend it? Do you have a plan?

How do *you* deal with Time? Are you even conscious of it? If you are, I bet you are constantly locked into either the future or the past. Relying on either memory or imagination.

Do you recognize these voices? "Once I get through this, I can have a drink . . . go on a vacation . . . retire." "I remember when I was young and doing landscaping was satisfying."

As you go to bed at midnight, are you thinking about waking up at seven a.m. so you can get to the office by eight a.m. so you can go to lunch by noon, because your software/pesticide people will be there at 1:30 p.m. and you've got a full schedule and a new client scheduled for 2:30?

Most of us are prisoners of the future or the past. While ping-ponging between the two, we miss the richest moments of our life—the present. Trapped forever in memory or imagination, we are strangers to the here and now. Our future is nothing more than an extension of our past, and the present is merely the background.

It's sobering to think that right now each of us is at a precise spot somewhere between the beginning of our Time (our birth) and the end of our Time (our death).

No wonder everyone frets about Time. What really terrifies us is that *we're using up our life and we can't stop it.*

It feels as if we're plummeting toward the end with nothing to break our free fall. Time is out of control! Understandably, this is horrifying, mostly because the real issue is not time with a small *t* but Death with a big *D*.

From the depths of our existential anxiety, we try to put Time in a different perspective—all the while pretending we can manage it.

We talk about Time as though it were something other than what it is. "Time is money," we announce, as though that explains it.

But what every landscape contractor should know is that Time is Life. And Time ends! Life ends!

The big, walloping, irresolvable problem is that *we don't know how much Time we have left.*

Do you feel the fear? Do you want to get over it?

Let's look at Time more seriously.

To fully grasp Time with a capital *T*, you have to ask the Big Question: *How do I wish to spend the rest of my Time?*

Because I can assure you that if you don't ask that Big Question with a big *Q*, you will forever be assailed by the little questions. You'll shrink the whole of your life to *this time* and the *next time* and the last time—all the while wondering, *What time is it?*

It's like running around the deck of a sinking ship worrying about where you left the keys to your cabin.

You must accept that you have only so much Time; that you're using up that Time second by precious second. And that your Time, your life, is the most valuable asset you have. Of course, you can use your Time any way you want. But unless you choose to use it as richly, as rewardingly, as excitingly, as intelligently, as *intentionally* as possible, you'll squander it and fail to appreciate it.

Indeed, if you are oblivious to the value of your Time, you'll commit the single greatest sin: You will live your life unconscious of it passing you by.

Until you deal with Time with a capital *T*, you'll worry about time with a small *t* until you have no Time—or life—left. Then your Time will be history—along with your life.

I can anticipate your question: If Time is the problem, why not just take on fewer clients? Well, that's certainly an option, but probably not necessary. I know a landscaper with a company that sees three times as many clients as the average, yet he doesn't work long hours. How is it possible?

This landscape contractor has a system. Roughly 50 percent of what needs to be communicated to clients is "downloaded" to the office staff. By using this expert system, the employees can do everything the landscape contractor or his subcontractors would do—everything that isn't landscape contractor-dependent.

Be vs. Do

Remember when you asked yourself, "What do I want to be when I grow up?" It was one of our biggest concerns as children.

Notice that the question isn't, "What do I want to *do* when I grow up?" It's "What do I want to *be?*"

Shakespeare wrote, "To be or not to be" not "To do or not to do."

But when you grow up, people always ask you, "What do you *do?*" How did the question change from *being* to *doing?* How did we miss the critical distinction between the two?

Even as children, we sensed the distinction. The real question we were asking was not *what* we would end up doing when we grew up, but *who* we would be.

We were talking about a *life* choice, not a *work* choice. We instinctively saw it as a matter of how we spend our Time, not what we do in time.

Look to children for guidance. I believe that as children we instinctively saw Time as life and tried to use it wisely. As children, we wanted to make a life choice, not a work choice. As children, we didn't know—or care—that work had to be done on time, on budget.

Until you see Time for what it really is—your life span—you will always ask the wrong question.

Until you embrace the whole of your Time and shape it accordingly, you will never be able to fully appreciate the moment.

Until you fully appreciate every second that comprises Time, you will never be sufficiently motivated to live those seconds fully.

Until you're sufficiently motivated to live those seconds fully, you will never see fit to change the way you are. You will never take the quality and sanctity of Time seriously.

And unless you take the sanctity of Time seriously, you will continue to struggle to catch up with something behind you. Your frustrations will mount as you try to snatch the second that just whisked by.

If you constantly fret about time with a small t, then big-T Time will blow right past you. And you'll miss the whole point, the real truth about Time: You can't manage it; you never could. You can only live it.

And so that leaves you with these questions: How do I live my life? How do I give significance to it? How can I be here now, in this moment?

Once you begin to ask these questions, you'll find yourself moving toward a much fuller, richer life. But if you continue to be caught up in the banal work you do every day, you're never going to find the time to take a deep breath, exhale, and be present in the now.

So let's talk about the subject of *work*. But first, let's find out what Tony has to say about time. ✤

CHAPTER 22

Six Minutes
of Time

Tony Bass

As if you could kill time without injuring eternity.
—Henry David Thoreau

B y this point in this book, you have gained a new appreciation for words. Michael's discussion of time with a capital *T* is one of the most enlightening concepts to which a small business owner could be introduced. I feel a great sense of comfort knowing that you have been introduced to the seriousness of *Time*—one word, two definitions.

As a landscape contracting business consultant, I get calls and questions from owners every day. Many of these questions arrive at a point when the owner is frustrated. Here are a few recurring questions:

- How can I get my crews to speed up?
- How can I get my estimates done faster?

- How can I stop wasting my time with the price-shopping homeowner?
- What equipment will really save me time in the field?
- Why can't my manager get as much done as I can?
- How can I process paperwork faster without flaws?
- How can I possibly take more vacations and get more accomplished?
- How can my business run without my having to be there all the time?
- How long will it take for me to build a multi-million dollar landscape enterprise?

As you can see, the questions revolve around time with a little *t*. Contractors get stuck on one or more issues. The benchmark for progress is often measured in time.

As I explained in chapters 14 and 20, time and motion studies are a necessary part of advancing the organization. Wise time use is indeed the responsibility of the business owner and management team. It can pay huge dividends. When you operate a landscape service business, every minute counts.

Six Minutes to Financial Prosperity

Let's explore the financial impact of wasted time. We'll start with a simple question: Is it possible that your employees waste as much as six minutes of time per day?

I have asked this question of seminar attendees more than two hundred times. Every time I ask this question, the answer is, "Yes, it is possible." There are times when the business owner, knowing what really happens out in the field, says, "It's not only possible, I know we easily waste six minutes per day per employee by stopping at the convenience store to get snacks."

I then say, "Okay, so you say it's possible. I would like to introduce you to a chart that places a price on the impact of just six minutes of wasted time. Let's see where your company falls on this chart today."

Here is how to find your company on this chart. First, estimate your employees' average wage by adding their hourly wages together, then divide that figure by their total number. Now locate the hourly rate closest to your company's in the chart's vertical axis. Follow it to the nearest number of employees in your firm on the chart's horizontal axis.

This figure will give you a good idea of your cost of just six little wasted minutes per day, per employee.

Estimated Annual Loss Caused By 6 Minutes of Wasted Time Per Employee Per Day						
Hourly Rate	days	# of Employees				
		3	5	7	10	15	20
$ 7.00	225	$ 945	$1,575	$2,205	$3,150	$4,725	$ 6,300
$ 7.50	225	$1,013	$1,688	$2,363	$3,375	$5,063	$ 6,750
$ 8.00	225	$1,080	$1,800	$2,520	$3,600	$5,400	$ 7,200
$ 8.50	225	$1,148	$1,913	$2,678	$3,825	$5,738	$ 7,650
$ 9.00	225	$1,215	$2,025	$2,835	$4,050	$6,075	$ 8,100
$ 9.50	225	$1,283	$2,138	$2,993	$4,275	$6,413	$ 8,550
$10.00	225	$1,350	$2,250	$3,150	$4,500	$6,750	$ 9,000
$10.50	225	$1,418	$2,363	$3,308	$4,725	$7,088	$ 9,450
$11.00	225	$1,485	$2,475	$3,465	$4,950	$7,425	$ 9,900
$11.50	225	$1,553	$2,588	$3,623	$5,175	$7,763	$10,350
$12.00	225	$1,620	$2,700	$3,780	$5,400	$8,100	$10,800
$12.50	225	$1,688	$2,813	$3,938	$5,625	$8,438	$11,250
$13.00	225	$1,755	$2,925	$4,095	$5,850	$8,775	$11,700

Time is expressed in dollars.

Please note: These calculations are based on 225 workdays in a year. Overhead was figured to equal the hourly rate. You may work more or you may work fewer days per year. Your overhead could be less or more than my estimates. But you get the point: Little minutes add up to big money.

As of this writing, the average US landscaping company has six or seven employees. If you have an average wage of $12 per hour you can estimate that six minutes of wasted time costs you $3,780 per year. How does this make you feel? Have you ever wondered where the profit in your business goes? You just found part of it. It's in your employees' pockets.

When I introduce this time management concept in seminars, I always get a chuckle out of the crowd. The notion of discovering a loss of $3,780 for a company with seven employees is significant, but not life changing. But then I change the parameters.

I ask, "How many hours do you work per day?" At times, I hear "eight hours per day." Others answer, "From sunup to sundown. We really push it during the season." Still others say, "Nine or ten hours." For the sake of math, let's compromise and say you work ten-hour days. Now I have one more question: Is it possible that in your firm, your employees waste as much as six minutes of time per hour?

Sheepishly, reluctantly, and with some hesitation, in almost every case, the attendees will agree, "Yes, it's possible that we waste as much as six minutes of time *per hour.*"

Let's go back to the chart for a moment. If it's possible that with your seven employees you are in fact wasting six minutes per hour, your annual loss in profits to your firm is *not* $3,780 but ten times greater, or $37,800 per year. And the crowd lets go with a deep and painful groan.

I was near Washington, DC for a seminar. The guy sitting in the front row owned and operated a company with fifty employees. We went through the process of calculating his estimated loss in profits from the chart above. He had an average wage of $11 per hour. We found the loss for a company with twenty employees and doubled it. Then we found the loss for ten employees and added this to get the total. We identified his six-minutes-per-day loss like this:

$9900 + $9900 + $4950 = $24,750 per year loss

When I returned to him to calculate the annual loss if his employees were wasting six minutes per hour, something amazing happened. He changed color. He was white as a sheet. He was sweating, and I was concerned that he had taken ill. It took less than sixty seconds to completely change his physical condition. Here is what he saw:

$24,750 x 10 = $247,500 per year loss

I asked him how he felt about the reality of looking a $247,500 loss in profitability in the face. He replied, "I think I'm gonna puke!"

The crowd got a laugh, but it was no laughing matter for the contractor sitting in the front row. His new level of awareness about the serious financial implications of squandered time was there to stay.

He sat up and listened attentively as I said, "Today's seminar is about putting systems into your business to help you and your team use time wisely, prevent confusion, and improve productivity. You see, ladies and gentlemen, locked in just six minutes of time per hour are the keys to financial prosperity. Little changes in how you operate can make a huge impact on your firm—six-figure impacts like we just learned."

I received an e-mail from the fifty-employee company owner a short time later. He thanked me for sharing the impact of just six minutes of time on his firm.

So far in this book, Michael and I have introduced you to a way of thinking and systems that can and will improve your landscaping company. No one wants to lose money in business. But it happens every day. The good news is it doesn't have to happen to *you* any longer. Your level of awareness has changed. And now that you understand the financial implications of time with a little *t*, we can get back to the bigger question of time with a capital *T*.

For you to have more *Time*, your business must grow. You can't do it all by yourself and build a company that has significant equity. Without the possibility of unlocking the money of equity, it is impractical to consider your operation more than a job.

Perhaps you operate a profitable company and it's like you have a well-paying job. Congratulations! But remember, the firm must take on a life of its own, a life that can be continued without your being there day in and day out. The life of the business continues.

Take a look at the photo below. I took this photo at one of my offices just two weeks before I sold my firm. I have included the photo here as inspiration to those of you who are somewhere in *Time*.

The elusive question is, "How do you do it? How do you find time to place systems in your company? How do you find time to work *on* the business? How do you grow to a point where the business takes on a life on its own? How do you add all those clients, employees, equipment, and vendors and work less?"

The answer is simple. "You must change *your* work."

Now let's see what Michael has to say about work. ✤

CHAPTER

23

On the Subject of Work

Michael E. Gerber

As we learn we always change, and so our perception. This changed perception then becomes a new Teacher inside each of us.

—Hyemeyohsts Storm

In the business world, as the saying goes, the entrepreneur knows something about everything, the technician knows everything about something, and the switchboard operator just knows everything.

In a landscaping company, landscapers see their natural work as the work of the technician. The Supreme Technician. Often to the exclusion of everything else.

After all, landscape contractors get zero preparation for working as a manager and spend no time thinking as an entrepreneur—those just aren't courses offered in today's schools and colleges of horticulture and landscaping. By the time they own their own landscaping company, they're just doing it, doing it, doing it.

At the same time, they want everything—freedom, respect, money. Most of all, they want to rid themselves of meddling bosses and start their own company. That way they can be their own boss and take home all the money. These landscape contractors are in the throes of an entrepreneurial seizure.

Landscape contractors who have been praised for their amazing skills believe they have what it takes to run a landscaping company. It's not unlike the plumber who becomes a contractor because he's a great plumber. Sure, he may be a great plumber—but it doesn't necessarily follow that he knows how to build a company that does this work.

It's the same for a landscape contractor. So many of them are surprised to wake up one morning and discover that they're nowhere near as equipped for owning their own company as they thought they were.

More than any other subject, work is the cause of obsessive-compulsive behavior by landscape contractors.

Work. You've got to do it every single day.

Work. If you fall behind, you'll pay for it.

Work. There's either too much or not enough.

So many landscape contractors describe work as what they do when they're busy. Some discriminate between the work they *could* be doing as landscape contractors and the work they *should* be doing as landscape contractors.

But according to the E-Myth, they're exactly the same thing. The work you *could* do and the work you *should* do as a landscape contractor are identical. Let me explain.

Strategic Work vs. Tactical Work

Landscape contractors can do only two kinds of work: strategic work and tactical work.

Tactical work is easier to understand because it's what almost every landscape contractor does almost every minute of every hour of every day. It's called getting the job done. It's called doing business.

Tactical work includes lawn mowing, edging, trimming, design, repairing, replacing and seeing clients.

The E-Myth says that tactical work is all the work landscape contractors find themselves doing in a landscaping company to *avoid* doing the strategic work.

"I'm too busy," most landscape contractors will tell you.

"How come nothing goes right unless I do it myself?" they complain in frustration.

Landscape contractors say these things when they're up to their ears in tactical work. But most landscape contractors don't understand that if they had done more strategic work, they would have less tactical work to do.

Landscape contractors are doing strategic work when they ask the following questions:

- Why am I a landscape contractor?
- What will my company look like when it's done?
- What must my company look, act, and feel like for it to compete successfully?
- What are the key indicators of my company?

Please note that I said landscape contractors *ask* these questions when they are doing strategic work. I didn't say these are the questions they necessarily answer.

That is the fundamental difference between strategic work and tactical work. Tactical work is all about *answers:* How to do this. How to do that.

Strategic work, in contrast, is all about *questions:* What company are we really in? Why are we in that company? Who specifically is our company determined to serve? When will I sell this company? How and where will this company be doing business when I sell it? And so forth.

Not that strategic questions don't have answers. Landscape contractors who commonly ask strategic questions know that once they ask such a question, they're already on their way to *envisioning* the answer. Question and answer are part of a whole. You can't find the right answer until you've asked the right question.

Tactical work is much easier because the question is always more obvious. In fact, you don't ask the tactical question; instead, the question arises from a result you need to get or from a problem you need to solve. Billing a client is tactical work. Designing a pond in a backyard is tactical work. Firing an employee is tactical work. Diagnosing plant disease is tactical work.

Tactical work is the stuff you do every day in your company. Strategic work is the stuff you plan to do to create an exceptional company/ business/enterprise.

In tactical work, the question comes from *out there* rather than *in here*. The tactical question is about something *outside* of you, whereas the strategic question is about something *inside* of you.

The tactical question is about something you *need* to do, whereas the strategic question is about something you *want* to do. *Want* versus *need*.

If tactical work consumes you,

- you are always reacting to something outside of you;
- your company runs you; you don't run it;
- your employees run you; you don't run them; and
- your life runs you; you don't run your life.

You must understand that the more strategic work you do, the more intentional your decisions, your business, and your life become. *Intention* is the byword of strategic work.

Everything on the outside begins to serve you, to serve your vision, rather than forcing you to serve it. Everything you need to do is congruent with what you *want* to do. It means you have a vision, an aim, a purpose, a strategy, an *envisioned* result.

Strategic work is the work you do to *design* your business, to design your life.

Tactical work is the work you do to *implement* the design created by strategic work.

Without strategic work, there is no design. Without strategic work, all that's left is keeping busy.

There's only one thing left to do. It's time to take action. And we'll do that right after Tony gives us his views on work. ✤

CHAPTER 24

Working for ...?

Tony Bass

We cannot solve our problems with the same level of thinking that created them.

—Albert Einstein

W hen we use the word *work* in relation to landscaping, we may think of "hard work" or "dirty work." But the reality is that the actual work of this industry is, for many, the most rewarding work in which you have ever participated. The impact on your soul when proudly looking at a freshly completed landscaping project is immeasurable.

The rewarding sounds of a satisfied customer's voice as you complete a lawn maintenance service visit can keep you moving forward in the hundred-degree heat of a summer's day. You flip the switch on the newly installed or repaired sprinkler system and watch the sprinkler heads pop up as water is carefully placed on the landscape. You smile. The weed-free lawn—lush, healthy, and

193

growing—just gets you excited. The world seems right when the trees are trimmed in a professional and orderly way. This is *our work*.

Your enthusiasm for *our work* probably got you into this business. But no matter how much you love the rewards listed above, if you can't support your family in a way that provides comfort, security, and harmony inside your home, you will leave this business.

There is simply too much at stake to think the joy of work will sustain you through too many years of "reinvesting profits into the business." At some point in time, as your family grows, your personal overhead grows, and the needs of your employees' families grow, you have to be making some real money. And this takes us back to *our work*.

I often get asked to speak to college and high school students about careers in the green industry. Young people sit attentively and listen as I share my experiences in building a career in an industry I love. Then we arrive at the time where the eager, soon-to-be graduates get to ask their questions. One of the most common questions is "Can you make more money with landscape design and installation, landscape maintenance, irrigation, lawn care, or some other specialty service?" The answer is that it matters less the type of work you do. It matters more how you choose to do it.

Michael makes a distinction between tactical work and strategic work. The reason most landscaping companies don't continue operating beyond the day the owner's back has given out is because the owners try to do too much tactical and not enough strategic work.

The seasonal nature of the landscape industry is a frequent excuse. We don't have training seminars during the spring because we are too busy with *our work*. We lay off employees in the winter because we don't have enough of *our work*. If you love getting your hands dirty, why not move to the opposite hemisphere each winter so you can stay busy with *our work*? Somewhere there is a garden to be built and weather that will allow it.

We can't really seek that kind of work year-round. The physical challenges of being outside in the elements—lifting, shoveling, walking, carrying, spraying, pruning, planting, and cleaning—is a real burden over time. We need the winter to relax and take some time off. The off-season is designed to rest up and recharge our batteries, you might say.

Human nature does not seek hard work. It's the difference between digging a hole four feet deep with a backhoe or with a shovel. Given the choice, most of us will use the backhoe to dig the hole.

Why do we choose work that is physically hard? Landscape technicians believe their work is done outside. Landscape managers believe their work is done outside interacting with crews and customers. Landscape company owners live by the mottos "Work is hard," "No pain, no gain," "No risk, no reward," and "Do it yourself if you want it done right." These beliefs hold you back and prevent you from focusing on your business's true potential.

As landscape businesses grow, some owners graduate from work in the field to managerial work. But for others, they simply graduate to the work of the office technician. I see landscape company owners ordering supplies, returning phone calls, going to the post office, making deposits at the bank, figuring time cards, entering data in the computer, spending hours in new employee interviews, running equipment repairs, and doing countless other tasks that keep them busy, busy, busy for ten to twelve hours per day. For what? Perhaps it is to avoid the fieldwork. Perhaps it is because they are addicted to being busy.

A recent client of mine wanted some help improving the amount of time from the prospect's initial request for a quote to the delivery of the completed quote. He had noticed a correlation between his company's sales success and the speed in which estimates were provided. Improving the speed of the quote process was a worthwhile goal for his firm. Pay careful attention. Speed pays handsome dividends.

We began by documenting his current process. And this is what we learned. The company did not have a system for the office staff to properly interview prospects on the phone, collect all relevant data, and move the caller several steps further along the sales process.

Here is the current process we documented. The prospect would call, and the office technician would answer the call. The prospect would leave his or her name, phone number, and address, and then wait twenty-four to forty-eight hours to be called back by a designer or estimator. This was because only the owner (also working as the sales-person) could set the schedule.

The office staff was not being used effectively, and the overall sales process had a built-in roadblock. Let's remove roadblocks from your business.

Let's talk about changing your work from tactical work to strategic work. The process starts with these simple questions:

- How do you spend most of your time?
- When is your peak performance time each day?
- What do you do during this time?

Each of us has a time of the day when our minds function on a higher level. For some, it is the morning, others midday, and for a few, afternoons and nighttime are when your mind is awake and full of energy. Use this time to do your strategic work. My recommendation is to discover the time of day—likely two to four hours in length—and set an appointment with yourself. Make a personal decision to keep this appointment and *work on your business* during your peak-performance time.

Establishing a routine that allows you to control this small swatch of time each day can transform your company. As Michael explains it, "Dream, Vision, Purpose, Mission." This is the strategic work of the entrepreneur and the business owner, not the technician. Your ideas must be put in writing to effectively communicate to those who will join you on your quest to accomplish the mission at hand. Hard work? This *is* hard work without practice. Just like using a skid loader or zero-turn mower for the first time is a little tricky, you begin to get better quickly with practice.

The landscape contracting industry continues to evolve. Our work is expanding into new and more highly specialized services. Will your mind be clear enough to discover these new services before your compet-itors do? It will if you are performing strategic work in your business. And if you do, there is unlimited potential for profits in an expanding landscape contracting business.

So it's really your choice. Hopefully, this book has given you a new level of awareness. Will you choose the work of the landscape technician, the office technician, the manager, or the entrepreneur *most of the time?* Choose technician work and your company stays small. Choose managerial work, and you stay busy. Choose entrepreneurial work and your business will grow.

But how can you really grow this company in your market area with all the competition and so few resources? This leads us to the next chapter. Thoughts become words. Your words lead to actions.

Now let's see what Michael has to say about taking action. ✤

CHAPTER 25

On the Subject of Taking Action

Michael E. Gerber

Deliberation is the work of many men. Action, of one alone.
—Charles de Gaulle

I t's time to get started, time to take action. Time to stop thinking about the old company and start thinking about the new company. It's not a matter of coming up with better companies; it's about reinventing the business of landscaping.

And the landscape contractor has to take personal responsibility for it.

That's you.

So sit up and pay attention!

You, the landscape contractor, have to be interested. You cannot abdicate accountability for the business of landscaping, the administration of landscaping, or the finance of landscaping.

Although the goal is to create systems into which landscape contractors can plug reasonably competent people—systems that allow the company to run without them—landscape contractors must take responsibility for that happening.

I can hear the chorus now: "But we're landscape contractors! We shouldn't have to know about this." To that I say: whatever. If you don't give a flip about your company, fine—close your mind to new knowledge and accountability. But if you want to succeed, then you'd better step up and take responsibility, and you'd better do it now.

All too often, landscape contractors take no responsibility for the business of landscaping but instead delegate tasks without any understanding of what it takes to do them, without any interest in what their people are actually doing, without any sense of what it feels like to be at the front desk when a client comes in and has to wait for forty-five minutes, and without any appreciation for the entity that is creating their livelihood.

Landscape contractors can open the portals of change in an instant. All you have to do is say, "I don't want to do it that way anymore." Saying it will begin to set you free—even though you don't yet understand what the company will look like after it's been reinvented.

This demands an intentional leap from the known into the unknown. It further demands that you live there—in the unknown—for a while. It means discarding the past, everything you once believed to be true.

Think of it as soaring rather than plunging.

Thought Control

You should now be clear about the need to organize your thoughts first, then your business. Because the organization of your thoughts is the foundation for the organization of your business.

If we try to organize our business without organizing our thoughts, we will fail to attack the problem.

We have seen that organization is not simply time management. Nor is it people management. Nor is it tidying up desks or alphabetizing client files. Organization is first, last, and always cleaning up the mess of our minds.

By learning how to *think* about the business of landscaping, by learning how to *think* about your priorities, and by learning how to *think* about your life, you'll prepare yourself to do righteous battle with the forces of failure.

Right thinking leads to right action—and now is the time to take action. Because it is only through action that you can translate thoughts into movement in the real world and, in the process, find fulfillment.

So first, *think* about what you want to do. Then *do* it. Only in this way will you be fulfilled.

How do you put the principles we've discussed in this book to work in your landscaping company? To find out, accompany me down the path once more by following these three steps:

1. *Create a story about your company.* Your our story should be an idealized version of your landscaping company, a vision of what the preeminent landscape contractor in your field should be, and why. Your story must become the very heart of your company. It must become the spirit that mobilizes it, as well as everyone who walks through the doors. Without this story, your company will be reduced to plain work.

2. *Organize your company so that it breathes life into your story.* Unless your company can faithfully replicate your story in action, it all becomes fiction. In that case, you'd be better off not telling your story at all. And without a story, you'd be better off leaving your company the way it is and just hoping for the best.

Here are some tips for organizing your landscaping company:
- Identify your company's key functions
- Identify the essential processes that link those functions
- Identify the results you have determined your company will produce
- Clearly state in writing how each phase will work

Take it step by step. Think of your company as a program, a piece of software, a system. It is a collaboration, a collection of processes dynamically interacting with one another.

Of course, your company is also people.

3. *Engage your people in the process.* Why is this the third step rather than the first? Because, contrary to the advice most business experts will give you, you must never engage your people in the process until you yourself are clear about what you intend to do.

The need for consensus is a disease of today's addled mind. It's a product of our troubled and confused times. When people don't know what to believe in, they often ask others to tell them. To ask is not to lead but to follow.

The prerequisite of sound leadership is first to know where you wish to go.

And so "What do *I* want?" becomes the first question, not "What do *they* want?" In your own company, the vision must first be yours. To follow another's vision is to abdicate your personal accountability, your leadership role, your true power.

In short, the role of leader cannot be delegated or shared. And without leadership, no landscaping company will ever succeed.

Despite what you have been told, win-win is a secondary step, not a primary one. The opposite of win-win is not necessarily "they lose."

Let's say "they" can win by choosing a good horse. The best choice will not be made by consensus. Asking, "Guys, what horse do you think we should ride?" will always lead to endless and worthless discussions. By the time you're done jawing, the horse will have already left the post.

Before you talk to your people about what you intend to do in your company and why you intend to do it, you need to reach agreement with yourself.

It's important to know (1) exactly what you want, (2) how you intend to proceed, (3) what's important to you and what isn't, and (4) what you want the company to be and how you want it to get there.

Once you have that agreement, it's critical that you engage your people in a discussion about what you intend to do and why. Be clear—both with yourself and with them.

The Story

The story is paramount because it is your vision. Tell it with passion and conviction. Tell it with precision. Never hurry a great story. Unveil it slowly. Don't mumble or show embarrassment. Never apologize or display false modesty. Look your audience in the eyes and tell your story as though it is the most important one they'll ever hear about business. Your business. The business into which you intend to pour your heart, your soul, your intelligence, your imagination, your time, your money, and your sweaty persistence.

Get into the storytelling zone. Behave as though it means everything to you. Show no equivocation when telling your story.

These tips are important because you're going to tell your story over and over—to clients, to new and old employees, to landscape contractors, to landscape subcontractors, to gardeners, and to your family and friends. You're going to tell it at your church or synagogue, to your card-playing or fishing buddies, and to organizations such as local garden clubs, chambers of commerce, or local colleges and technical schools.

There are few moments in your life when telling a great story about a great business is inappropriate.

If it is to be persuasive, you must love your story. Do you think Walt Disney loved his Disneyland story? Or Ray Kroc his McDonald's story? What about Fred Smith at Federal Express? Or Debbie Fields at Mrs. Fields Cookies? Or Tom Watson Jr. at IBM?

Do you think these people loved their stories? Do you think others loved (and *still* love) to hear them? I daresay *all* successful entrepreneurs have loved the story of their business. Because that's what true entrepreneurs do. They tell stories that come to life in the form of their business.

Remember: A great story never fails. A great story is always a joy to hear.

In summary, you first need to clarify, both for yourself and for your people, your company's *story*. Then you need to detail the *process* your company must go through to make your story become reality.

I call this the business development process. Others call it reengineering, continuous improvement, reinventing your company, or total quality management.

Whatever you call it, you must take three distinct steps to succeed:

- *Innovation*. Continue to find better ways of doing what you do.
- *Quantification*. Quantify the impact of these improvements on your company.
- *Orchestration*. Orchestrate this better way of running your company so it becomes your standard, to be repeated time and again.

In this way, the system works—no matter who's using it. And you've built a company that works consistently, predictably, and systematically. It will be a company you can depend on to operate exactly as promised, every single time.

Your vision, your people, your process—all linked.

A superior landscaping company is a creation of your imagination, a product of your mind. So fire it up and get started like Tony did. He'll tell you about it in the next chapter. ✤

CHAPTER 26

So, What's Next? Taking Action

Tony Bass

The way to get started is to quit talking and begin doing.
—Walt Disney

Some say that education is the new form of currency. The more you know, the more you earn. This book is a great start in expanding your education. However, if this book sits on a shelf and these new ideas are not transformed into words, and those words are not organized into actions, things will not improve for you. The world is moving quickly; it will leave behind those who do not keep up. Education *is* the new form of currency, but if it is not invested—put into action—nothing happens.

There is no better upside in life than owning a well-organized business. You are in an elite club as a business owner. Your business is the one place where you're in control. You get to make the rules. I suggest that you create the rules in your favor. Let's get started by reinventing your company, the place where you spend the majority of your time doing what you love to do. Think about the potential.

Small Steps

Have you heard of the Betty Crocker company? It's famous for its boxed cake mixes. This company figured that people could make a great tasting cake if they start with just the right ingredients, mix them in the right order, place these ingredients in the right size pan, place them in the oven at the right temperature, and remove the pan at precisely the right time, followed by a certain amount of time to cool and the final touches of frosting and decorations. The system works perfectly.

The company taught this system in cookbooks, over the radio airwaves, and, yes, right on the back of the cake mix box. The system was refined, refined again, and perfected. Suddenly anyone could create great tasting, evenly moist, perfectly sized, and nicely decorated cakes. The history of baking cakes would be altered forever into the future. The process became the product. No more guesswork. Cooking success became easier, with less work and greater consistency.

What in the world does this have to do with birthing, reinventing, or expanding a landscaping company? Everything! What the Betty Crocker company did for the homemaker and cooking, *The E-Myth* does for your business. The solution is in the system.

My dream is that every landscape company owner worldwide can avoid the mistakes and pain caused by operating a broken business. My dream is that you can take your landscaping company and transform it to a moneymaking machine that serves you instead of you serving it. My dream is that you and your family will learn how to unlock the true potential of your landscape company regardless of where you live and who works there. Simply stated, my dream is to help you master the landscape business.

Start with your dream. How does your landscaping company look in your dream? Why does your company exist? Whom does it serve? What services does it provide? Why do people need those services? How will it provide those services? When do people need those services? How many people will be required to perform those services? What steps will be involved to make certain the products and services are provided as promised? How will you attract clients? How will you price services? How will you expand services? Small questions. Big challenge.

A word of caution. This is not an exercise for your team; at least, not at first. You must start with *your dream*. You must start with *your life*. You must get clarity on *your vision*. You must clearly articulate *your purpose* inside of you before you define the mission outside of you. This begins as a personal matter. Don't start by asking your team for a brainstorming session on the future. This will come later.

Action Options

This takes me back to the very beginning of this book. When I read *The E-Myth* for the first time, I faced a life dilemma. In an instant, I knew the old business was broken and in need of massive overhaul. In the next instant, I knew the overhaul would be a major process and require a completely different approach to my daily work. But how? How do you take action and avoid mistakes?

Here are three ways to take action:

- **Simply follow the instructions in this book**. Go back to chapter 1. As you read, create what Michael and I have described. Although we could not cover every last detail within the scope of the book, the major steps are here, and in the right order. It's just like baking a cake. However, unlike baking a cake, real money is at risk. Don't make many mistakes or you may go broke on the way to growing old.

- **Join a professional landscaping or business education association.** Attend their professional business meetings, educational programs, and seminar events. Better yet, volunteer to work within the association and help guide the direction of future education within the organization. Get involved in the landscape industry on a higher level by networking with peers. But before you take advice from peers, ask to see their financial statements!

- **Seek a coach (or consultant) to help guide you through the process.** This way, if you begin to get off course, your coach can help get you back on track. The best part of having a coach is that your education will move at a pace that matches your ability. The coach will adjust your actions and help you clear your mind when day-to-day clutter clouds it. Having a business coach is one of the secrets to success for high-achieving individuals. There are lots of business coaches but there are only handfuls who have actually built landscape companies from scratch to multi-million dollar enterprises. Seek advice from someone who actually has a track record of landscape business ownership. Nothing replaces "been there, done that."

From the options above, the third option is the shortest distance between where you are and where you want to go. In my own life, each time I have tempered my goals with an experienced coach's influence, I have accelerated my progress and made fewer mistakes. And you can too.

Let's go back for a moment and think about Betty Crocker. Can you bake a cake if you are given step-by-step instructions? How about if I give you the exact supplies in exactly the right amounts? What if I coach you on the sequence of events? What if I provide pictures of the final product to inspire you on how it will turn out? Can you do it? Yes, you can, but only if you take the smallest of steps in the right order.

I want you to think about your company as the perfect little cake on the front of that cake mix box. Every time you walk by the cake mix display at the grocery store, think about your business and its potential. Each time you attend a birthday party, look at the cake and think about your company and its potential to take on a unique shape, color, and purpose. The occasions may change, but the cake is always there, adding to the moment.

Your Company

After working with hundreds of landscaping companies, I have found a clear pattern in their development. What exists in the owner's mind is played out in the company. If the owner thinks his company can earn a 20 percent profit, it will. If the owner thinks the firm needs a new facility, it will be built. If the owner thinks this business is fiercely competitive and only the lowest prices win bids, then that is what he will find everywhere he goes. If he thinks employees are a pain in the butt, they always will be. If he thinks he must do everything himself to get it done right, he will be correct. If he thinks he can't control his schedule, he won't be able to. It's amazing!

Think about your company's future. Do you see yourself standing in front of a success story? Do you see your clients giving praise for all you have done for them? Do you see your team standing proudly with you? Do you see your employees enjoying the fruits of their labor? What are you thinking right now? Are you thinking expansion or contraction? Are you thinking abundance or scarcity? What you think of most of the time becomes your reality.

What is the single greatest challenge facing your company today? There is an answer to this challenge—it is found within the pages of this book. Growth will get you past this challenge. Business growth and personal growth are your friends.

And there will be another challenge around the corner. The bigger the problem, the bigger the opportunity to grow as you solve the problem. Small people solve small problems. Big people solve big problems. Are you small or are you big? Most are traveling through life somewhere between small and big, somewhere between young and old, and somewhere between a landscape company of scarcity and a landscape company of abundance. Where are you right now?

I hope to see you on the road to an abundant life. I hope to see you on the road to making your landscape company one that you can't believe until you see it. And I hope you will share my story with others you encounter along the way. Like Michael says, "Everyone loves a great story."

And your story is just getting started. If you're stuck, we can help. If you've achieved your impossible dream, share it. Contact us. We want to hear about you and your landscape business success. ✤

AFTERWORD

Michael E. Gerber

For more than three decades, I've applied the E-Myth principles I've shared with you in this book to the successful development of thousands of small businesses throughout the world. Many have been landscaping companies—contractors specializing in everything from landscape design and landscape construction to property maintenance and lawn care.

Few rewards are greater than seeing these E-Myth principles improve the work and lives of so many people. Those rewards include seeing these changes:

- Lack of clarity—clarified
- Lack of organization—organized
- Lack of direction—shaped into a path that is clearly, lovingly, passionately pursued
- Lack of money or money poorly managed—money understood instead of coveted; created instead of chased; wisely spent or invested instead of squandered
- Lack of committed people—transformed into a cohesive community working in harmony toward a common goal; discovering each other and themselves in the process; all the while expanding their understanding, their know-how, their interest, their attention

After working with so many landscape contractors, I know that a company can be much more than what most become. I also know that nothing is preventing you from making your company all that it can be. It takes only desire and the perseverance to see it through.

In this book—another in the E-Myth Expert series—the E-Myth principles have been complemented and enriched by stories from Tony, a real-life landscape contractor who has put these principles to use in his company. Tony had the desire and perseverance to achieve success beyond his wildest dreams. Now you can join him.

I hope this book has helped you clear your vision and set your sights on a very bright future.

To your company!

ABOUT THE AUTHORS

Michael E. Gerber

Michael E. Gerber is the legend behind the E-Myth series of books, which includes *The E-Myth Revisited*, *E-Myth Mastery*, *The E-Myth Manager*, *The E-Myth Enterprise* and *Awakening the Entrepreneur Within*. Collectively, his books have sold millions of copies worldwide. He is the founder of In the Dreaming Room™, a 2½-day process to awaken the entrepreneur within, and Origination, which trains facilitators to assist entrepreneurs in growing "turnkey" businesses. He is chairman of the Michael E. Gerber Companies. A highly sought-after speaker and consultant, he has trained more than tens of thousands of clients, and has millions of readers. Michael lives with his wife, Luz Delia, in Carlsbad, California.

ABOUT THE AUTHORS

Tony Bass

Tony Bass is an entrepreneur, inventor, author, consultant, and speaker whose passion is helping landscape contractors achieve their fullest potential.

He built Bass Custom Landscapes from scratch, sold it for a seven-figure profit, and retired at age forty-one. The high-efficiency Super Lawn Trucks™ system Tony invented for his company is now used by contractors in forty-two U.S. states and Canada. He has produced several audio and video training programs and five books, including *The Money Making Secrets of a Multi-Million Dollar Landscape Contractor*, a three-book set purchased by thousands. His personal consultations and seminars receive rave reviews.

Tony lives with his wife, Lynn, and their children, Holly and Maxx, in Warner Robins, Georgia.

ABOUT THE SERIES

The E-Myth Expert series brings Michael E. Gerber's proven E-Myth philosophy to a wide variety of different professional business areas. The E-Myth, short for "Entrepreneurial Myth," is simple: Too many small businesses fail to grow because their leaders think like technicians, not entrepreneurs. Gerber's approach gives small enterprise leaders practical, proven methods that have already helped transform tens of thousands of businesses. Let the E-Myth Expert series boost your professional business today!

Books in the series include:
The E-Myth Attorney
The E-Myth Accountant
The E-Myth Optometrist
The E-Myth Chiropractor
The E-Myth Financial Advisor
The E-Myth Landscape Contractor

Forthcoming books in the series include:
The E-Myth Architect
The E-Myth Real Estate Brokerage
The E-Myth Real Estate Investor
The E-Myth Insurance Store
. . . and 300 more industries and professions

Learn more at: www.michaelegerber.com/co-author

Have you created an E-Myth enterprise? Would you like to become a co-author of an E-Myth book in your industry? Go to www.michaelegerber.com/co-author.

THE MICHAEL E. GERBER
ENTREPRENEUR'S LIBRARY
It Keeps Growing...

Thank you for reading another E-Myth Vertical book.

Who do you know who is an expert in their industry?

Who has applied The E-Myth to the improvement of their practice as Tony Bass has?

Who can add immense value to others in his or her industry by sharing what he or she has learned?

Please share this book with that individual and share that individual with us.

We at Michael E. Gerber Companies are determined to transform the state of small business and entrepreneurship worldwide. *You can help.*

To find out more, email us at Michael E. Gerber Partners, at gerber@michaelegerber.com.

To find out how YOU can apply the E-Myth to YOUR practice, contact us at gerber@michaelegerber.com.

Thank you for living your Dream, and changing the world.

Authors of Business Design

Michael E. Gerber, Co-Founder/Chairman
Michael E. Gerber Companies™
Creator of The E-Myth Evolution™
P.O. Box 131195, Carlsbad, CA 92013
760-752-1812 O • 760-752-9926 F
gerber@michaelegerber.com
www.michaelegerber.com

Join The Evolution^{SM}

Find the latest updates:
www.michaelegerber.com

Attend the Dreaming Room Trainings
www.michaelegerber.com

Listen to the Michael E. Gerber Radio Show
www.blogtalkradio.com/michaelegerber

Watch the latest videos
www.youtube.com/michaelegerber

Connect on LinkedIn
www.linkedin.com/in/michaelegerber

Connect on Facebook
www.facebook.com/MichaelEGerberCo

Follow on Twitter
http://twitter.com/michaelegerber

CPSIA information can be obtained at www.ICGtesting.com
Printed in the USA
LVOW132008140213

320012LV00001B/1/P